# Perfect
# Relaxation

**Elaine van der Zeil**

BOOKS

Published by Random House Books 2009

1 2 3 4 5 6 7 8 9 10

First published in Great Britain in 2009 by
Random House Books

Random House, 20 Vauxhall Bridge Road,
London SW1V 2SA
www.rbooks.co.uk

Addresses for companies within The Random House Group Limited
can be found at: www.randomhouse.co.uk/offices.htm

The Random House Group Limited Reg. No. 954009

A CIP catalogue record for this book
is available from the British Library

ISBN 9781847945570

The Random House Group Limited supports The Forest Stewardship
Council (FSC), the leading international forest certification organisation.
All our titles that are printed on Greenpeace approved FSC certified paper
carry the FSC logo. Our paper procurement policy can be found at
www.rbooks.co.uk/environment

Typeset by SX Composing DTP, Rayleigh, Essex
Printed and bound in Great Britain by
CPI Bookmarque, Croydon, CR0 4TD

**Perfect Relaxation**

Elaine van der Zeil is a consultant who seeks to help people
achieve their full potential and maintain work/life balance. She
runs workshops and provides coaching in stress management
and communication skills.

Other titles in the *Perfect* series

# Contents

## Quick Reference Section

This book is dedicated to Pete

# Introduction

Life today is full of demands. At times they feel overwhelming. When we don't feel in control, we feel stressed and anxious. This book is about living a happier, fuller life. It is about appreciating the good things and overcoming the bad with least hassle. It isn't just about lying down on the floor and breathing, or taking a well deserved holiday, it's much, much more. The word 'relaxation' is used in its widest sense: the sense of being at ease with yourself and others in all sorts of situations. It's about living joyfully in the present instead of harking back to past hurts and injustices, or worrying about the future. It could just as well be called 'Perfect BEING', for that's just about what it covers.

The person doesn't exist who hasn't experienced difficulty in dealing with someone or something in his or her life. These difficulties can cause stress. At its best, stress is a healthy challenge which tests your mettle and develops you. At its worst, it saps your energy and it can be a killer. Whatever your levels of healthy or unhealthy stress, buying this book is one way of helping yourself to feel more relaxed and to lead a more energetic and peaceful life, with YOU in control.

Stress is a much used word these days. It's all around us – at work, at school, at home – and the causes are infinite. Exams, working with fewer staff, meeting deadlines, the demands of technology, managing a family, illnesses, losses, coping with relationship problems, staying young and beautiful . . . and lots more. These are some of the issues which cause anxiety, irritation, anger . . . and all the things which are the opposite of relaxation. Before you can deal with the stress you feel when you get into an anxious or wound up state, it helps to understand what stress is and what it does to you. And why it affects some people more than others. You'll find this in part 1.

Stress can make you ill; it can cause alarming symptoms – physical, mental and emotional. The good news is you can do something about it! You can take back some control – and you can keep it. Part 2 is a stimulating collection of strategies which you can adopt to prevent stresses which are avoidable and to counteract those which are not. Having some of these strategies will help you to feel relaxed and secure – and to *enjoy* life.

This is a self-help book. You can read it from cover to cover if that's your style. But you don't have to. Dip in if you prefer. However you choose to read it, and whatever your state of mind, emotion or health, there's something relevant in here for you. You'll be trying some new approaches. And you'll be exploring your potential to be more creative and fulfilled. It has been exciting for me to write it. I hope that my excitement will be shared by you in your discoveries about yourself.

It's a smallish book so you can keep it with you. It'll remind you that there are things you can do to help yourself in the car, at home, on a train journey, at work, at the bus stop, in the supermarket – anywhere.

# Part one

# Understanding relaxation and what gets in the way

# 1 Getting to know yourself

We'll start off by looking at the typical things which get in your way when you want to feel relaxed. You can have a good look at them, understand them better, then put them into perspective or get rid of them altogether. It might help to have by your side a notebook and pen as you read. You'll be invited to jot down some thoughts about your personal triggers and responses to potentially stressful events, which you can reflect on.

The most laid back and hardy of us feels anxious from time to time. Who can truthfully say that at some time they have not faced unexpected problems, relationship difficulties, losses, challenges which have seemed insurmountable, or felt just plain scared at the prospect of making a speech or going through an interview for school, college or a job?

Think of a recent experience which stressed you out. It may have been something fairly small, or it may have been a major life event – a bereavement, job loss, an argument with a friend, a computer breakdown, yet another traffic jam. Whatever it was, just think of the effect it had on you.

First of all, what was your mental state during and after this stressful experience? What were you thinking? How did that event affect your capacity to think and concentrate normally? Did you feel muddled or confused? Was your memory affected? Or your judgement? Self-confidence? Jot down anything you noticed.

Next, think of the emotional effect. How did it make you feel? Irritable? Anxious? Guilty? Hostile? Weepy? Moody or insecure? What happened to those feelings as you went through the experience?

Next, the physical effects. What did you notice about your body which was different from usual? Headaches, butterflies, racing pulse? Shakiness, coldness, sweatiness, diarrhoea, constipation? Tense and aching muscles? If so, where?

Don't worry about getting things in the right category. Just jot them down anyway.

Are there any other observations you can make about yourself when you are under stress? Do you smoke more? Drink? Bite your nails? Jiggle your fingers? Drive recklessly?

This is the start of your learning about yourself.

## Why bother to relax? Isn't stress inevitable?

Of course lots of things will happen in your life to prevent you feeling relaxed and happy. We all experience feelings of having too much to do in too little time, we have to cope with illnesses – ours and those of our family and friends – moving home, finding a job, dealing with children . . . all potentially stressful situations. The list is endless. But you can learn to take these in your stride. By dealing with your stress and using it constructively, you can conserve and channel your energies into achieving peace of mind and making positive changes where you can, instead of wasting your resources on worrying and fighting against things you can't change. You will be learning new skills which, just like riding a bicycle, will come to you automatically when you need them. The important thing is that you are **in control.** You make choices about how to take back control, when it feels as if life is controlling you. As a result:

- you feel fitter
- you feel happier
- you sleep better
- you get fewer illnesses
- you have more energy and motivation
- you feel more relaxed
- you can take on more and still feel in control
- your relationships improve
- you are secure in yourself
- you thrive.

You and others around you will notice the difference.

## How stressed are you?

Put a tick in the appropriate box

| HOW OFTEN DO YOU . . . | OFTEN | SOMETIMES | NEVER |
|---|---|---|---|
| Feel irritable? | | | |
| Talk fast? | | | |
| Become confused? | | | |
| Forget things? | | | |
| Think negative thoughts? | | | |
| Have marked mood swings? | | | |
| Feel weepy? | | | |
| Drink too much? | | | |
| Eat too much? | | | |
| Skip meals? | | | |
| Feel rushed? | | | |
| Feel that you have no energy? | | | |
| Have difficulty getting to sleep? | | | |
| Wake up early? | | | |
| Feel angry? | | | |
| Worry about the future? | | | |
| Dwell on the past? | | | |
| Lose your concentration? | | | |
| Smoke? | | | |
| Have emotional outbursts? | | | |
| Take tranquilizers? | | | |
| Feel you can't cope? | | | |

You may want to come back to this questionnaire and fill it in again, when you've had an opportunity to understand and tackle the things which prevent you relaxing and enjoying your life.

# 2 What is this thing called stress?

What does the word mean to you? Take a few minutes to think about some words which come to your mind when you think of stress. Hassle, overload, anxiety, worry, tension, nervousness, trauma, strain, burden, angst, shock, desperation, oppression. You may have some others which sum it up for you.

We tend to think of all the negative words which sum up how we feel when we are overwhelmed by feelings of inadequacy; when we believe we're not coping as well as we should. (Watch out for this word 'should' – we'll come back to it later and look at how our 'shoulds' dictate to us.)

> Stress results from a *belief* that you can't cope successfully and it causes you unpleasant physical, mental or emotional reactions.

The important thing about this definition is that it emphasises what you *believe*, not necessarily *what is*. To illustrate my point, just think back a few years to a time when you were faced with a really difficult situation. Maybe a death in the family, financial difficulties, a child's illness, or someone losing a job. Would you have *believed* before, or at the time, that you could have coped and come through it? Perhaps not. And yet here you are, reading this book, proving that you came through that, and possibly many more difficulties since then. Maybe you deserve a pat on the back right now – so give yourself one.

But think about some of those unpleasant reactions – physical, mental and emotional – and be sure that by the time you have reached the end of this book, you'll have a box of tricks to help you minimise them day to day or the next time you are faced with a particularly stressful situation.

## Pick 'n' mix

We all react differently to stress; some people bottle it up, others can't stop talking. Some get indigestion, others get headaches or skin rashes, some of us drink more than is good for us. We don't even react to the same things. One person can dread going to the dentist; another takes it in his or her stride. One can happily watch a spider crawling across the floor; another screams and stands on a chair. One finds a six-mile jog therapeutic; another would find it extremely stressful, even to contemplate.

When it comes to dealing with stressors, because we are so wonderfully unique, what works for one doesn't necessarily work for another. So this book contains lots of different suggestions, some of which will work better for you than others. Try them all, or as many as are practicable for you. Have a go at some you've not tried before.

> *I did it my way*
> Frank Sinatra, singer and actor, 1915–1998

## Positive and negative stress

Stress isn't always negative. Think of the stress you put yourself under when you go for an interview, compete in a sports event, take an exam, speak in public, move house, enrol in a language class, or learn to dance. In these ways and many more, you give yourself stress or pressure, so that you can achieve something for yourself.

So it's helpful to think of two different kinds of stress – positive and negative. Alternatively, some people think in terms of pressure (positive) and stress (negative), or stress and distress. Because we'll talk a lot about positive things in this book, we'll stick to the distinction between positive and negative stress and, on the whole, when we talk just of 'stress', it'll be the negative kind, the kind you'll want to reduce or get rid of.

Stress is Positive when *You're* in control
Stress is Negative when *It's* in control

## Taking or losing control

You've already thought of some circumstances in which you felt you were unable to cope. Chances are they were circumstances which had been forced on you, uninvited. Often these negative stressors are things which are out of your control. For human beings, there is very little worse than not having control over your own life and your own destiny. US studies of air force personnel in the war showed that the co-pilots, not the pilots, suffered the most stress on flying missions. The reason for this is that they had no control over the direction or speed of the aircraft, no power over the decision-making process which jeopardised their lives. The pilots suffered less stress because they had control. If you think of some of the most stressful situations you have experienced, they will often be those when you were in a state of uncertainty, where someone else was making decisions on your behalf – about your job, your family, your finances, your housing. Not knowing the news can be worse than having bad news. At least bad news is definite, and you know what you have to cope with.

## The Performance Curve

So let's look at the effects of positive and negative stress. Peter Nixon, a cardiologist from Charing Cross Hospital, came up with the idea of a Human Function Curve, or Performance Curve, to help us understand our stress levels. See Figure 1.

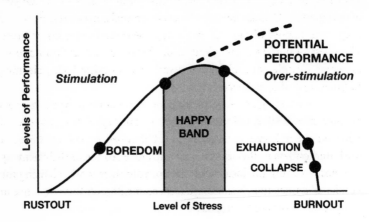

*Figure 1. The Performance Curve*

Let's look at the curve in more detail.

## Rust-out

Confucius said that sitting in a comfortable chair doing nothing is wonderful for two minutes. Even two hours. After two days it is neither wonderful nor comfortable.

Boredom or 'rust-out' is stressful. You've probably heard of experiments in which volunteers are suspended in warm water for lengthy periods of time, to experience sensory deprivation – no touch, sight, sound, taste or smell. In those situations, though they may feel comfortably warm, people experience the stress of having no stimulation and, in extreme cases, they begin to hallucinate, to create their own internal stimulation to replace what's lacking in their environment. These experiments prove that we cannot survive and thrive without activity of the body and mind to interest and challenge us.

Rust-out can apply to people who have retired from work, who have no hobbies or interests to fill their days. Or to young mothers who miss the stimulation of adult company while looking after their new baby.

They may feel negative stress – the uncomfortable kind – through lack of stimulation. Human beings, like other animals, need stimulation to keep them happy. Without it they can show disturbing signs of stress. The stress of boredom can result in uncharacteristic behaviours too – extremes include compulsive handwashing, checking locks, cleaning routines, fear of open spaces, panic attacks.

If you are feeling bored, you strive for stimulation to bring you to a happier frame of mind in which you can experience a sense of achievement, at home, at work, at play. Often people who are bored at work find outlets in their social life which give release to their pent-up energies – leading the local scout group, voluntary work, chairing the Residents' Association, becoming a local councillor. Or they are active in competitive sports or local groups.

## The happy band

As you become more stimulated, putting more demands on yourself, and coping with them successfully, you feel happier because you feel a sense of achievement. In this state you feel in control, energetic, active, alert and ready for anything. Your energy levels increase because you feel good about yourself and what you're doing. You seek out challenges, like taking up a new sport, looking for a more responsible job, learning computer skills, or offering your services to the local community. When you're stimulated and excited you'll find more and more energy to do what you want and need to do, and you'll thrive on it. Feel the buzz!

## Burn-out

Then as you take on more and more, you may begin to feel over-stimulated, particularly if you are faced with demands which you don't choose, like bereavements, illnesses, divorce, changes at work. You begin to feel overwhelmed, unable to cope, life gets on top of you. You get into the 'burn-out' state and if you don't do anything about it, this can lead to exhaustion and collapse, either mental or physical. Think of someone you know who has had a collapse, seemingly caused by a very small trigger. That's because they were already well on the way down the performance curve – and then comes the last straw.

## Where are you on the curve?

The trick is to stay in the happy band, and to notice when you're beginning to get dangerously close to its limits. Are you feeling bored and fed up? Or are you rushing around and starting to panic? If you are on the left-hand side of the curve, look for new and enjoyable ways to increase your stimulation. If you are on the right-hand side of the curve, this isn't the time to be changing your job, moving house, or becoming a Samaritan. Work on your existing stress levels first, regain your energy, move back to the happy band, and then look for the new challenges. Then you can climb even higher on a new performance curve (see dotted line on figure 1).

Having too few or too many demands on you causes stress. The negative kind. Finding just the right amount of stimulation is like tuning the strings of an instrument. Too slack and the music will be out of tune. Too tight and the chances are the strings will snap. Just right and you'll feel in tune with your mind and body and others will appreciate the beautiful music too!

Learning how to spot stress and its symptoms will make you aware of where you are on the curve. The strategies covered in Part two will help you to move forwards or backwards into that healthy happy band. By adopting good stress management tactics, you can increase your personal Performance Curve to higher and higher levels.

Take a few moments to put a cross on the curve where you feel you are now. Where were you on the curve this morning? On Monday? Last Saturday night? After your last holiday? A year ago? What does this tell you about your stress levels?

## Stress and life events

Two physicians, Doctors Holmes and Rahe, carried out studies of stress levels in their patients and found some interesting correlations between exposure to negative stress over a twelve-month period and immediate likelihood of illness.

| LIFE EVENTS IN PAST 12 MONTHS | SCORE |
| --- | --- |
| Death of a partner | 100 |
| Divorce | 73 |
| Separation from partner | 65 |
| Jail sentence or being institutionalised | 63 |
| Death of close family member | 63 |
| Personal illness or injury | 53 |
| Marriage | 50 |
| Loss of job | 47 |
| Marriage/partner reconciliation | 45 |
| Retirement | 45 |
| Health problem in close family | 44 |
| Pregnancy | 40 |
| Sex problems | 39 |
| Addition to family | 39 |
| Major changes at work | 39 |

| LIFE EVENTS IN PAST 12 MONTHS | SCORE |
|---|---|
| Changes of financial status | 39 |
| Death of a friend | 37 |
| Changes in line of work | 36 |
| Changes in number of disagreements with partner | 35 |
| Large mortgage taken out | 31 |
| Mortgage or loan foreclosed | 30 |
| Responsibility change | 29 |
| Child leaves home | 29 |
| In-law problems | 29 |
| Personal achievement realised | 28 |
| Partner starts or stops work | 26 |
| Starting a new school | 26 |
| Leaving school/college | 26 |
| Changes in living conditions | 25 |
| Changes in personal habits | 24 |
| Trouble with employer | 23 |
| Change in working hours | 20 |
| Change in residence | 20 |
| Change in recreation | 19 |
| Change in church/spiritual activities | 19 |
| Change in social activities | 18 |
| Small mortgage taken out | 17 |

| LIFE EVENTS IN PAST 12 MONTHS | SCORE |
|---|---|
| Change in sleeping habits | 16 |
| Changes in number of family get-togethers | 15 |
| Major change in eating pattern | 15 |
| Holiday | 13 |
| Christmas | 12 |
| Minor violation of the law | 11 |

Your total =
150–199 points increases your likelihood of illness by 40%
200–299 points increases your likelihood of illness by 50%
300 points and over increases your likelihood of illness by 80%

Source: Holmes and Rahe 'Scaling of Life Events', *Journal of Psychosomatic Research*, 1967

Though the scale is not new, psychologists agree that it has stood the test of time, and still represents many of our major stresses. Add in your own if you feel there are any missing and estimate a score based on its effect on you. Then read through the list and tick the lifestyle changes you have experienced in the last twelve months. Total up the points and check your score against the groups below. The points indicate your potential risk of becoming ill as a result of the stresses placed on you. Bear in mind that we all respond differently to certain types of stress, so this is not an absolute measure. It is, however, a useful indicator and may surprise you.

It would be impossible for you to try to completely avoid any of these life events. They come to all of us in time. The important thing is – if you have a high score, be extra kind to yourself, at least for a time, until your score goes down. You may, for example, decide to wait a while before taking on a new stressful experience like moving house, or changing your job – unless of course either of these are likely to *reduce* your stress levels in a relatively short time.

## Exercise

Make a list of the things which are giving you negative stress right now (hassling, debilitating things which sap your energy – it feels like THEY are in control).

You'll identify ways to deal with them as you read on. Which one do you want to tackle first?

Now list the things which give you positive stress (exciting, challenging things which give you a buzz – with YOU firmly in control).

Can you identify one which you can give yourself more of right now?

# 3 **What stress does to you**

Imagine Ned, our caveman ancestor, ekeing out an existence for his family around the mouth of his cave, hunting for his food and being hunted in return by whatever hairy predator happened to be passing. At the sight of a snarling hungry bear, a chain of events would be set up in Ned's body to help him to deal with the threat. This chain of events would help him either to face the beast and fight him off, or to run like mad for the nearest cover. Hence *Fight & Flight.* This same chain of events happens in all of us to this day, and is common to all animals. While you're reading this, just take a minute to think how you have felt when you've been crossing a road and suddenly a car has come out of nowhere and is hurtling towards you. Or when you're alone in the house at night and suddenly you hear an unexpected noise.

For Ned, as for all of us in a dangerous situation today, the sight or sound (or smell) of the threat, in Ned's case the bear, triggers off an alarm button in the brain. This alarm button is the hypothalamus. It sets up a chain of events which send a sudden surge of energy all round your body to equip you for enhanced performance. The hypothalamus sends messages to the adrenal glands, which start to pump adrenaline round the body. Your mind and body goes into a state of red alert to enable you to take some swift, drastic action to save yourself.

Let's start at the top. Your *brain* becomes super-sensitive to all information passing through it. If you've ever been in an accident, or near-accident, you may have experienced a feeling that everything is happening in slow motion. This is your brain going into overdrive. You take in every detail of what's happening and a second can seem like a minute. So you are able to think more quickly than normal how you might get out of the situation.

The pupils of your *eyes* suddenly dilate, so that you have extra peripheral vision. Ned might find this very useful if he is being chased by a bear, and is able to spot a friendly cave-mouth out of the corner of his eye. Just as you would want to spot the gate in the field if you were being chased by an angry bull.

The *muscles* of your shoulders, arms, back and legs tense, ready for action. Fists clench and the muscles of the jaw, mouth and forehead tense, in anticipation of fighting or running away. The *blood supply* to the muscles increases, so that they will be more effective. Blood, and the oxygen and glucose it carries, fuels the muscles and fuel needs to be in plentiful supply. In addition, *blood clotting* mechanisms become heightened, anticipating injury. The *heart* beats faster to increase the flow of blood to the needy muscles, and blood pressure rises. The rate of *breathing* increases, to enable the body to take in more oxygen to fuel the muscles.

The *liver* releases stores of fat into the bloodstream which are broken down to help in the fuelling process. These stores of fat are commonly recognised as cholesterol. The *digestion* slows down or stops, as the blood supply is redirected to the muscles of the back, the arms and the legs. While Ned is fighting the bear or running away from it, his digestion takes second place to his muscular strength and agility. The *colon* is starved of blood and cannot perform its normal functions. Constipation may be the result. Or the bowels are suddenly emptied to lighten the body and make fight and flight easier.

Your *immune system* stops working. It isn't essential that you are protected from colds and flu while you are being chased by that bull. Your body has far more important things to tackle. *Sweating* takes place, to reduce body temperature.

Adrenaline acts like an accelerator to keep your body going at peak rate. What's happening here is that your Sympathetic Nervous System swings into action, automatically and involuntarily to help you deal with personal danger. And what a wonderful mechanism it is! You've heard stories of what people have achieved in a highly charged stressful situation, seeming to use super-human resources – the mother who lifts a car to release her trapped daughter, the fireman who holds up a collapsing ceiling while rescuers save the victims, non-runners who run long distances to get help in an emergency.

Let's return to Ned and the bear and suppose that Ned has successfully killed it or chased it away, or has run out of its path to safety. The finger comes off the alarm button, and the state of red alert stops. Now the Parasympathetic Nervous System begins to return the mind and body to their normal resting state. Muscles relax, the blood supply returns to other parts of the body, breathing becomes calmer and deeper, the body cools down, and the immune system makes its comeback. The adrenaline levels drop, the body regains its balance and can set about its day to day physical and mental repairs. All is well and life goes on at the normal pace.

Like Ned, you respond to threats and dangers by pressing your own alarm button and going through this vast range of reactions. Today, most of the threats we face are not six feet tall, hairy and growling. They are more likely to be the demands of trying to do too much, answering other people's needs, meeting targets, coping with difficult relationships . . . and so on. But your body responds in the same way. And because so many of the threats which face us are with us day in, day out, we don't give our Parasympathetic Nervous System a chance to return us back to a normal resting state. Instead of fight or flight, we sit and stew. So the wear and tear on our minds and bodies is immense!

It's important to understand this physical fight and flight response, because if you understand it you can do something about it. Deliberately taking calmer, deeper breaths and practising relaxation techniques can help your Parasympathetic Nervous System to restore your body to its equilibrium. This is why physical and mental relaxation are so important in beating stress.

How many of your stress symptoms can you identify with the *Fight & Flight* response? Indigestion? Headaches? Bad back? Sweating? Aching jaw? Neck strain? Butterflies in the tummy? Diarrhoea?

Make a rough sketch of your body. Where do you feel the stress most? Put an X on any part of the body where it affects you or make a list of the ways in which your body tells you all is not well. This is the first stage in developing your awareness of your personal stress points. These are the areas to concentrate your positive energies on more and more each day, so that you can deliberately relax those tensions away and feel progressively healthier, happier and more able to cope.

## Your immune system

Have you ever wondered why it is that you always feel ill at the weekend or, for those of you who don't have a Monday to Friday job, when you take a few days off work? People often complain that their holidays are spoiled by colds, flu, or some other virus which catches them unawares when they are trying to relax. Think of the immune system and what happens to it when you are under stress. It stops performing effectively. Your adrenaline keeps your body and mind in a state of tension, so that you can deal with the problems you have to face and, in effect, it puts off any illness which you might be heading for, postpones it until you can *afford the time* to be ill. So you go on holiday or take a weekend off, and wham! The adrenaline levels start to drop and you begin to relax. But the immune system takes a while to get going again, and there's a gap. Your adrenaline isn't working for you any more, but your immune system hasn't quite caught up. There's an immunity gap, and this is when you are susceptible to all sorts of illnesses.

## Adrenaline addiction

You might be addicted to the feeling of adrenaline coursing round your system, and imagine that something is not quite right if it stops. Or maybe you are too afraid to stand still for a moment for fear of what might happen to you if you haven't got 101 things on your busy schedule. You hear people say, 'I thrive on stress and I couldn't possibly be happy if I wasn't completely overloaded.' This constitutes adrenaline addiction. It is a physical addiction, just like a need for drugs, and it is based on messages you are giving yourself about not being a valuable person unless you are working your socks off.

If you recognise yourself as an addict, you may also recognise feelings of depression and anxiety during the first few days (or all!) of a holiday. Many people have said to me, 'There I am, in this beautiful cottage in the middle of the country, the sun is shining, all I have to do is walk to the nearest shop for the picnic lunch and the bottle of wine – and I feel so depressed and miserable, because I don't have to chase around like a maniac . . . What's wrong with me? . . . My family and friends can't understand why I'm irritable and moody and neither can I . . . I've been looking forward to the break, and then I can't enjoy it . . . I can't relax . . . Things start to get better after a week or ten days, then it's time to go back to work . . .'

Keeping your adrenaline levels at a more healthy level from day to day will help you enjoy your free time better, enabling you to switch off more quickly after a working day or week.

## Your cholesterol levels

Because your body mobilises fats into your bloodstream when you are under threat, your cholesterol levels rocket during that time. Prolonged stress keeps your levels high. Research has shown that you can control only 25% of your cholesterol through a good diet, the other 75% gets there through stress. Eating tuna sandwiches on brown bread with no butter is fine – but it doesn't make up for getting rid of some of that stress!

## The fright response

Sometimes, you may respond to a sudden stressful situation by freezing on the spot. You're not able to take action at all. You might feel like a rabbit trapped in the headlights of a car, feeling a sense of impending doom, but unable to move. This is a variation of *Fight & Flight*. Your body and mind can't choose whether to run or whether to stay and fight, and this sets up an immobilisation of the whole system. Sensible relaxation and stress management strategies will help to ensure that you don't find yourself in this frightening situation.

> *We are not disturbed by things, but by the view we take of things*
> Epictetus, philosopher, 55–135 AD

## The vicious circle of stress

Think of your mind and body as a closed loop, like the Circle Line on the London Underground. If there's a blockage at Edgware Road, the trains at Liverpool Street will be affected. In just the same way, when your body is tense (shoulder muscles, jaw, forehead furrowed ready for fight or flight) your brain is receiving messages that things are not well down there. Your face, hands and feet are jam-packed full of sensors which feed information back to the brain, telling it if things are hot, cold, solid, liquid, slimy, hairy, etc. They also feed information back about the level of activity. If you jiggle your fingers a lot or grind your teeth, tap your feet rapidly or fidget constantly, you are sending messages to your brain which say that you are very disturbed, anxious and apprehensive. Those messages keep the finger well and truly pressed on the alarm button.

So by deliberately quietening and stilling your body, you will be telling your brain that things are not that bad, and are improving every second. This will have the effect of releasing the finger from the alarm button.

Similarly, if you are constantly telling yourself, through your internal dialogue or your dealings with other people, that you are afraid, inadequate and can't cope – 'Oh I've *never* been able to deal with figures . . .', 'Dogs *terrify* me . . .', 'I *should* be able to do three things at once . . .', 'I *can't* bother anyone else with this . . .' – the alarm button sends the body into a frenzy of activity to deal with the anticipated threat. It might not even be something you can identify, like the monthly bills, noisy neighbours, a job interview or work overload. It may simply be a feeling of doom, which contributes to a vicious circle of stress, and sets up even more strong alarm reactions in your body. So replacing negative thoughts with positive ones can help you to break into the vicious circle and restore your body and mind to a more relaxed state. More of that later.

When something has caused you stress, or maybe you have been conditioned – 'Mother was terrified of spiders and so am I' – the alarm response it sets off reinforces your fear. You can make your own symptoms worse by telling yourself, 'Every time I see a spider I *freak out.*' Then of course you will. Even a picture of a spider, or the thought of one, will press the alarm button.

## Some results of prolonged stress

There are so many stress-related illnesses that we could fill the book. These are just some of the things people experience when they don't relax and keep their life in balance: insomnia, heart disease, allergies, asthma, panic attacks, depression, migraine, stomach ulcers, muscular aches and pains, nervous breakdown, diabetes, viral illnesses, nervous eczema, backache, diarrhoea, heartburn, irritable bowel syndrome, digestive disorders, cancer, arthritis.

You may have experienced some of these yourself. You can understand now why this happens – it's often years of wear and tear on the body that's constantly in a state of red alert, where the Parasympathetic Nervous System never gets a chance to restore you to a peaceful state of mind and body. It's an alarming list, but don't get stressed out by it! The fact that you have bought or borrowed this book means you are doing something about it, showing a healthy response to the stress you have recognised in yourself. You'll be better equipped to prevent it in future.

# 4 Stress, relaxation and personality types

In the 1950s, in the USA, two cardiologists, Doctors Friedman and Roseman, were having their waiting room redecorated. The redecoration included re-upholstering the chairs, which had seen better days. A chance remark by the upholsterer set them thinking. 'Why is it,' he said, 'that all the chairs are worn threadbare at the front edge, while the cloth at the back of the seats is barely touched?'

The two doctors carried out some research on what type of person used their practice, and based their work on the hypothesis that maybe some types of person were more susceptible to heart disease than others. Clearly their patients did a lot of fidgeting and shuffling on the edge of their seats. Their studies led them to conclude that there were two main personality types, Type A and Type B, and that the vast majority of cases with whom they dealt were Type A.

> *One of the symptoms of an approaching nervous breakdown is the belief that one's work is terribly important*
> Bertrand Russell, philosopher, 1872–1970

## The Type A personality

These were individuals who were identified as being very hard-driving, both of themselves and of others, ambitious, competitive and task-orientated. The Type A personality is likely to be rushed, trying to achieve a great deal in a very short time, is aggressive, critical, impatient and sets high standards for self and others – not just dedicated, but obsessed. This person will often do several things at once, shaving and reading a map while driving, for example, or taking business calls on the golf course – if he/she ever allows themself any time off for such leisure pursuits. The Type A personality can be hostile under pressure, easily alienating those who try to provide support. This may include family and work colleagues, whom the Type A person will tend to blame when things go wrong. When things go right, he will claim the credit. You will see the Type A person sitting in a traffic jam on the motorway, tooting his horn, banging his fists on the dashboard, mouthing obscenities to no one in particular, blaming the car in front/the government of the day/the person he is going to see/the family for making him late, drumming his fingers on the steering wheel, and looking like thunder.

The Type A personality will often be much more wrapped up in himself than in anyone else and may show little interest in the problems or needs of others. When others tell him about their problems he will give them minimum attention, will dismiss them lightly and expect them to 'get on with it'. In a work situation, getting the task done quickly will be all-important. So explaining in detail why things need to be done will not be a high priority; when this results in misunderstanding or ineffective solutions, he will think people incompetent and slow-witted. Many Type As do not feel really alive unless they are locked in conflict with someone or something – overcoming bigger and bigger challenges. Winning is everything. Recognise him/her?

It's not all bad. On the plus side, Type A personalities are often highly motivated, physically and mentally alert, good at spotting and seizing opportunities and carrying along others who have not as much energy and commitment. They will make good initiators of action, and will persevere under adverse conditions to achieve their goal. They will be the Conquerors of Everest and the business tycoons, though they may, at their extremes, be poor team players, needing to get to the top at the expense of others rather than with their co-operation. It is not the Type A personality itself which causes illness, but rather the feelings of anger, hostility and distrust which are associated with it.

## The Type B personality

This type is laid back, co-operative, calm, unhurried, not particularly ambitious, friendly and tolerant. The Type B person will not set impossibly high standards for him/herself nor for others, but will 'go with the flow' and will take a philosophical view of life's seeming unfairnesses. Contrary to expectations, these people can also achieve a great deal, by calmly and patiently dealing with each situation in turn and maintaining good supportive relationships. Unlike the Type A person, they will reward others with praise, will take account of personal problems and will make allowances for individual inadequacies.

In the same motorway traffic jam, the Type B person will be having a stretch, getting himself comfortable, listening to his favourite tape or programme on the radio, smiling or chatting to a neighbouring motorist and making the most of his unexpected break.

In essence the Type A person seems to be saying, 'I am only worth what I can achieve – and others have to recognise me in order to give me value.' They put increasing pressure on themselves and on others and can get into a stress spiral as their expectations of what they should achieve grow, and their ability to cope with more lessens. Exhaustion and collapse are the results. The Doctors' research goes a long way to explaining the worn-out chairs in the waiting room and the heart attacks outside it.

> *Sometimes it is not enough to do our best; we must do*
> *what is required*
> Sir Winston Churchill, politician, 1874–1965

# Which personality type are you?

Give yourself a score between 6 and 0 on the following statements where 6 = very much like me, 3 = neutral, 0 = not like me at all:

- I always feel rushed
- I walk fast
- I am competitive
- I am impatient
- I go all out with whatever I am doing
- I have few or no interests outside work
- I hide my feelings
- I talk fast
- I try to do more than one thing at a time
- I drive myself and others, hard
- I finish people's sentences for them
- I am forceful in speech
- I want recognition from others
- I eat quickly
- I am ambitious
- I look ahead to see the next task.

Your score will fall somewhere between 0 and 96. The higher your score, the more typical of *Type A* you are; the lower your score, the more typical of *Type B*. Don't worry too much about the absolute score, just be aware where you are on the line and which type you favour. Maybe you score differently at home and in the workplace. What does that tell you about yourself?

There are thousands of ways you can take back control over your life and deal effectively with those situations which give you grief and hassle. In the next part of the book we will look at a series of strategies you can adopt to make your life easier and happier.

Part two

# Finding new ways to relax and beat stress

# 5 Change your body - change your mind

Back to the London Underground. The mind and the body are totally interconnected in an ongoing, never-ending loop. What happens in one is reflected in the other. This chapter looks at a number of different ways in which you can relax your body. When you do that, you will automatically be changing the state of your mind. Don't take my word for it. Try it and experience for yourself that it works!

## Physical relaxation and breathing

Relaxation is a learned skill. Once you master it, it will automatically click into place to help you deal calmly and effectively with difficult situations.

Many people who are terrified of spiders, wide open spaces, lifts, dogs, and any number of ordinary, everyday events, have found themselves debilitated, often to extremes, by their irrational fears. Some become afraid to leave their homes, or to go into a supermarket, or to visit a friend with a pet. The quality of their lives is decreased by their response to a given stimulus. That response could be a result of years of conditioning – being brought up in a house where a parent was terrified of mice or 'creepy-crawlies'. Or it may be a result of a bad experience they have suffered personally – being bitten by a dog, or being afraid to go out alone because they were once mugged in a park. Many have been helped to overcome their terror by learning to use physical and mental relaxation techniques when they meet the object of their fear. You can do this too, and you don't need to have an extreme response – it can just be ongoing stress and feelings of tiredness and general anxiety which make you a less effective person.

The secret is to relax both your body and your mind, and to bring your system back to a healthy, comfortable state where your body functions normally, not on red alert.

'So how do I relax?' some of you will be saying. 'And what possible chance do I get with the demands made on me, at home, at work . . . etc . . . etc . .?' 'I can't spend two hours every morning sitting cross-legged gazing at my navel . . .'

Well, you don't have to. Practising relaxation is like learning to drive a car. It takes a bit of effort to start with, when you're not used to it, but if you keep practising, just for short periods, it'll become as natural to you as steering or changing gear. You won't realise you're doing it, but you'll feel so much better. Your energy levels will increase, you'll achieve more in the time available and you'll make yourself and others feel the benefit. Master the skill of relaxation and it will repay you for the rest of your life.

The next part of the book is a series of relaxation exercises you can do to help you feel calmer and more confident. Some are very short, some a bit longer. You can try them all and see which ones work best for you. They're set out so that you can choose one no matter what time you have or what place you're in.

If it's helpful, think of them as ways of lifting the lid on the pressure cooker as it's building up a head of steam and about to burst the pan. Just little lifts at regular intervals will keep the kitchen and everyone in it, safe.


## When you have ten seconds

### The Emergency Stop Breath (for use any time)

This is my version of a very useful technique which I learned when I was training to be a teacher of relaxation. This technique lets you break quickly into the vicious circle of stress at any time of the day. When you feel yourself getting hassled, just take a moment and breathe out sharply. Make a 'HOOW sound and make it as noisy as you like. Get rid of that breath in the bottom of your lungs. Then take an easy gentle breath in. Think 'eeeeeeasy' as you breathe. Then breathe out s-l-o-w-l-y with a breathy 'oooooh' sound until you've emptied your lungs. Let your shoulders drop right down. Do this a couple of times and you'll instantly feel calmer. You're bringing your body back into equilibrium.

## When you have half a minute

### Palming

This is easy to do and only takes a moment. Rub your hands together vigorously to create heat and energy. Place the ball of your hands over your closed eyes, fingers resting on your head. Rest your elbows on a surface if there's one available. Drop your shoulders and let go. Feel the energy transferring from your palms to your eyes and brain. Breathe easily and gently and enjoy the feeling of warmth and darkness. After a spell of concentrated effort, this will relax the eyes and neck.

## When you have a minute

### Alternate nostril breathing

This is very calming. Sit comfortably. Place the index, middle and ring finger of your right hand on your forehead. Rest the thumb and little finger gently on each side of the nose. Gently close your eyes if you wish, or gaze dreamily at a spot in your near view. Now inhale. Close the right nostril with your thumb. Exhale through the left nostril, and then allow the breath to enter the left nostril and be drawn down into the lungs. When the inhalation is complete, pause, then close the left nostril with the little finger and open the right nostril. Now exhale. Inhale through the right nostril and when the breath is complete, pause and close the right nostril with the thumb. Open the left nostril. Exhale.

Repeat the process twice more.

Start off with three alternate breaths and gradually build it up. Doing this for just a few moments every day will help you retain a new balance, calmness and stillness.

## When you have two minutes

### Diaphragmatic breathing

Sit comfortably and drop your shoulders. Take your attention to your breathing and notice the rhythm. Then place one hand on your upper chest and one below your ribs. Begin to lengthen your breath, allowing the out-breath to empty your lungs. Breathe in gently and notice how the area under your ribs expands as you inhale. Breathe out slowly and fully, allowing your waist area to contract naturally. Pause for a moment and repeat five times. Your upper hand should not be moving at all, as the movement of the air should be felt in the diaphragm, not in the upper chest. If you do feel a rise and fall in the chest, deliberately push out your waist and tummy as you breathe in and feel the difference in your lung capacity. Imagine the breath working through a pair of bellows with the wide end below your waist and the narrow end behind your nostrils.

## When you have five minutes

### Seated relaxation

Sit well back in a firm chair which supports your body – not an armchair, which allows it to slump. Place your feet firmly on the floor, or on a cushion if you have short legs or a tall chair! Rest the palms of your hands on your thighs. Now really *think* about the next instructions. Pause after each sentence and concentrate. Take your time.

Think of your spine lengthening and the spaces between the vertebrae becoming larger. Lengthen your neck and bring your chin parallel to the floor. Soften your jaw and allow your forehead to smooth over.

Now allow your shoulders to drop away from your ears. Feel the space between the shoulders and ears getting longer as your shoulders give in to the pull of gravity. Notice how the neck lengthens again. Imagine that a silver thread is gently pulling the crown of your head up towards the sky.

Close your eyes and begin to lengthen your breath. Focus your attention on the abdominal area, and allow the incoming breath to go right down to the bottom of your stomach. Your lower body should expand outwards as the breath enters. Don't worry about looking inelegant. Then feel the breath filling up the whole of the central tunnel of your body, from your nostrils down through the back of your throat into your chest and lungs. The lungs are like crumpled fabric – stretched out they cover the area of a tennis court – so they are capable of expanding to take in lots of air.

Hold the breath for the count of five, then breathe out slowly. This is a complete Yogic breath. If you have never been used to breathing deeply, it may make you feel slightly dizzy, so try just one to begin with. When you get used to it, try a number and feel the soothing, calming and stilling of the mind and body.

## When you have ten minutes

### Standing relaxation

This can be really helpful when you're standing waiting for a bus, or in some other queue. Practise it at home first so that you know what to do without any prompting. Don't worry about drawing attention to yourself. No one need know what you are doing.

First of all *stand well*. How? Place your feet shoulder-width apart, with your toes pointing forwards – not sideways. Feel the ground beneath all parts of your feet – the big toes, the balls of the feet, the sides, the heels. Wriggle your feet until you feel evenly balanced. This stabilises you and gives you a solid base for relaxing the rest of your body.

Next notice your knees. Are they jammed together in tension? Allow them to feel soft and warm. Let go of unnecessary tension. Feel the muscles at the backs of the knees letting go and moving downward and outward with gravity. Keep just enough tension to maintain your steady standing posture. Release the muscles of the thighs. Now your buttocks. Give up any tension which isn't strictly necessary to keep you steady. Allow the large muscle of each buttock to let go. Soften the base of your spine.

Bring your attention to your stomach. Pull the tummy muscles in gently, to give support to your lower back. Feel your spine straightening and lifting towards the sky as the upper part of your body is gently supported by the strong and steady base you have created.

Release the tension in your shoulders. Feel the space between your shoulders and your ears increasing as gravity pulls your shoulders down. Imagine you are carrying two heavy shopping bags. Feel them pulling your shoulders down. Then keep that feeling as you let the bags go. Your arms hang heavily by your sides. Your fingers are loosely curved and you feel them lengthening and relaxing.

Notice the back of your neck, how it is loosening and straightening. Feel the extra space which this creates in your upper back. With your chin parallel to the floor, loosen your jaw. Feel it soft and easy. Allow the muscles of your temples and the sockets round your eyes to rest and slacken. Feel your forehead becoming higher and wider. Imagine a magnet pulling the crown of your head gently upwards, lengthening the space between the vertebrae of your neck and upper back.

Breathe gently and easily, and then begin to extend the breath gradually. Breathe in for a count of four. Hold for a count of four – notice the stillness. Breathe out for a count of four, then hold for a count of four.

Repeat ten times. Then allow your breathing to become easy and relaxed. If there is any strain with this exercise, then count only two on each of the holds until you feel you can comfortably manage four.

# When you have half an hour or more

## Longer, deeper relaxation

This relaxation is for when you have a period of thirty minutes or so. It progressively relaxes different parts of your body, and then introduces you to a mind-focusing technique which you may find useful at other times. Wear loose, comfortable clothes and choose a warm room. If any part of your body feels chilly, you'll find it difficult to relax. The temperature of your body drops as you lie down, so you might want to use a blanket to keep a nice even warmth. In Yoga classes, many of us got into our sleeping bags for maximum cosiness! Make sure that you are not going to be disturbed. If possible, ask a friend or partner to take you through the exercise, quite slowly, reading the instructions below. This allows you to take in the relaxation completely, without disturbing yourself to read it. You can do the same for your partner after you've benefitted from the experience. Ready?

Lie down on the floor with a book or slim cushion under your head. Experiment until you find one that's just the right height off the floor so that your head feels comfortable, and your spine is one continuous line from your shoulders to the base of your head. It's important to have your head neither thrown back nor propped forward.

You might want to put pillows under your arms and/or knees to make you even more comfortable. Experiment and use whatever suits you best. Above all, pamper yourself. This part of the exercise shouldn't be rushed, as it is the first stage of complete relaxation.

Lie down so that your body is symmetrical, with the backs of your hands on the floor. Wriggle about until your are sure that the left side is a mirror image of the right. Let your body flop. You could be a rag doll or a jelly that's not quite set. Visualise an imaginary line running down the exact centre of your body, from head to toes, and feel the right and left sides dropping away from each other as gravity pulls you down into the floor. Gently close your eyes.

Allow your breath to leave your body until you have emptied your lungs. Breathe in gently and evenly through your nose, noticing how the breath feels as it enters your nostrils. As you breathe out, through your mouth, allow any tension to sink down into the floor. Repeat this for five breaths, noticing each time you breathe out that your body is getting heavier and sinking more deeply into the floor.

Now turn your attention to your body. First your feet. Concentrate on your toes, which are floppy and warm. Then the ankles, which turn out towards the floor. Notice how they roll away from each other as you let go and allow yourself to sink down. Notice the backs of your legs, which are resting heavily on the ground. They feel warm and soft. Your thighs are rolling away from each other, heavy and floppy on the floor. Allow the muscles in your legs to let go and give themselves up to the floor.

Let the feeling of warmth and heaviness spread to your buttocks and pelvis. They flop comfortably and loosely on the floor. Allow any residue of tension to sink down into the floor and disappear.

Bring your attention to your back and allow the spine to sink. The floor is supporting you fully, and you don't need to use any muscles to hold yourself there. Allow your abdominal muscles to become soft and loose and to sink towards your spine. Notice your breath, even and calm, rising and falling gently in your abdominal area.

Think of the fingers of your hands. They are lying loosely curved, without tension. Your wrists flop heavily onto the floor and the warmth and heaviness travel up into the elbow and the upper arm. Next, your shoulders. Allow them to sink right down into the floor, and to sink further still as you surrender your body to the floor and allow it to spread gently under you.

Your neck is resting gently at the back, and there is a feeling of space and softness. As your head rests on the cushion you feel it getting heavier. Any leftover tension is allowed to melt away beneath you.

Gently bring your attention to your face. Notice your jaw, which so often retains tension. Allow your jaw to become soft and floppy, as if it were made of thick liquid or jelly. Pay particular attention to how your jaw feels as you release tension. Note the sensation of letting go in this area. Your lips are soft and slightly parted. Your tongue flops loosely in your mouth. Your cheeks flop outwards with gravity towards the floor as you let go. Notice your eyes, which rest easily and heavily in their sockets, without tension. And your forehead, which becomes smooth and wide and peaceful.

Become aware of your whole body again, and take your attention to any part which can flop and relax even more. Allow it to sink. Let it go.

Notice your breath, still and gentle, even and tranquil. Feel it entering your nostrils again, and be aware that with each in-breath there comes energy which moves into every part of your body. With each out-breath, you let go of tension and sink down even further into a deep and refreshing relaxation.

Breathe in energy . . . Breathe out tension . . .

Take a few moments to concentrate on this energising experience. When you are ready, gently begin to lengthen and deepen your breath. After five breaths, begin to wriggle your fingers and toes, getting yourself ready to move. Then stretch your feet and your hands and arms. Pull up your knees towards your body, feet flat on the floor. Roll over onto your side. Gradually open your eyes. Then gently push yourself up off the floor to a sitting position. Get up completely when you are ready. Don't rush the recovery – be gentle with yourself – keep the feeling of relaxation. Have a stretch and a yawn.

You can develop the benefit of this relaxation by associating it with a word, 'calm', perhaps, or 'easy'. Or something more unusual – 'Tenerife' or 'sailboat' – anything which conjures up a pleasant picture or feeling. Say your word to yourself at various points in the relaxation exercise, including the beginning and the end. When you feel yourself getting hassled, say your word and it will take you back into your relaxed state.

A good relaxation session can replenish your body more effectively than sleep. Giving yourself regular periods of relaxation can help you feel calm, refreshed and alert.

## What I notice about myself when I relax

Jot down your observations about parts of your body which relax easily, parts of your body which you need to concentrate on to relax more, and how you feel mentally and emotionally when you relax your body.

## Mind-focusing techniques

The suggestion that you concentrate on *breathing in energy* and *breathing out tension* is a mind-focusing or meditative technique which, once you are relaxed in your body, brings a deeper sense of peace to the mind. There are many things you can concentrate on to have the desired effect. Try some different ones and see which works best for you.

- Listen to the sounds inside and outside the room.
- Imagine you are gazing at your favourite flower.
- Notice your thoughts as they drift through your mind. Think of them as passing clouds, and watch as they come into view and fade away.
- Count each breath as it enters and leaves your body.
- Concentrate on the central area of your forehead above your eyes. This is the 'Third Eye' in meditation, the eye which gives you insights into yourself.
- Concentrate on breathing in through your nose, feeling the breath pass down your body and out through your feet. Visualise warmth as you breathe out through your feet. This is an excellent technique if you suffer from cold feet and chillblains. People who practise this technique report that it actually warms their feet on cold winter nights. You can practise breathing through your hands, or through any part of your body which needs warmth. Persevere, it may not happen straightaway.
- Visualise a warm golden glow, in your solar plexus, behind your stomach, as you breathe in. Feel the solar warmth – think of the energy of the sun – and the glow spreading through your whole body from the central radiating point each time you breathe out.
- Mentally repeat a word or phrase over and over to yourself. Some like to repeat 'ohm' or 'peace', but you can say anything which brings you a feeling of inner calm. My Yoga teacher

used to have us think 'So' on the in-breath and 'Haam' on the out-breath. This was very relaxing.

- Think of your favourite colour, and imagine you are bathed in a blanket of coloured light. Or in a bubble of that colour, floating off into the universe.
- Visit your mental refuge – somewhere real or fictitious where you experience feelings of peace, calm and happiness. It could be a beach, a landscape, a favourite room, a lazy boat trip, an underwater scene.

If you've enjoyed doing some of these exercises and would like to learn and practise some more, treat yourself to a course of relaxation classes at your local college or gym.

## Taking exercise

Research shows that as you get older, people who take physical exercise remain more mentally alert as well as more relaxed than those who do not. Exercise enhances a positive mood and decreases anxiety and tension. In particular, people suffering depression and low self-esteem report great benefits from a regular exercise programme which includes vigorous physical activity.

Fitness can be defined as the ability to deal with your environment – so for some, you might need to be able to run a mile – for others that won't be the case. The secret is, finding the exercise which suits you, mentally and emotionally as well as physically, and doing it regularly.

Not only does exercise keep your body active and toned, but it releases endorphins, the body's natural pain-killing hormones, which make you feel good. People who exercise a great deal and for long periods report a feeling of being on a high – like a drug-induced state, which brings powerful feelings of well-being and euphoria. Yet unlike a drug, which can have negative side-effects, the release of the body's natural hormones can only do you good. The added benefit is that you are distracted from normal day to day problems, while you concentrate on a completely different activity, so helping you to feel refreshed and relaxed, ready to fight another day.

You don't have to go to extremes. Running marathons or jogging to work every day may not be your scene. Exercise your common sense as well as your body. I have seen a number of extremely fit friends experience serious problems with knee cartilages and various bone and muscle difficulties simply through overworking their bodies. So I recommend moderation in all exercise regimes.

> *One of the most pleasing sounds of springtime, to be heard all over the country, is the contented cooing of osteopaths as Man picks up his garden spade*
> Oliver Pritchett, journalist

Find something you really enjoy – it doesn't much matter what it is – rather than going with the latest trend of step aerobics or trampolining if that isn't really your style.

Even the most hard-working person can afford a small amount of money and some of their valuable time to spend on things which will help to develop their ability to deal with pressure/stress and make them fit and well-balanced individuals. See the list on page 41.

## Stretching

Athletes know the importance of flexibility. Stretching exercises form part of the workout for runners, swimmers, and most sportspeople. Vigorous exercise on contracted muscles can lead to injury and pain, hence the need to relax and stretch out the muscles before taking exercise. Go back to the section on *Fight & Flight* and think of the body's reaction to stress: all that tensing and stiffness which comes when you feel under threat. And the vicious circle, which reminds your mind how bad you feel and sets up a reaction which makes you feel even more tense and stiff.

## An exercise exercise

Find out what you really enjoy – here are some activities which will enhance your fitness and health. Think about them. Which of them do you enjoy/have you enjoyed at some time in your life? Put a tick against the activities.

| ACTIVITY | I ENJOY | I DO IT OFTEN | I DO IT SOMETIMES | I NEVER DO IT |
|---|---|---|---|---|
| Aerobics | | | | |
| Badminton | | | | |
| Bowling | | | | |
| Canoeing | | | | |
| Climbing | | | | |
| Cricket | | | | |
| Dancing | | | | |
| Cycling | | | | |
| Fencing | | | | |
| Fishing | | | | |
| Football | | | | |
| Gardening | | | | |
| Golf | | | | |
| Horse riding | | | | |
| Jogging | | | | |
| Karate | | | | |
| Kickboxing | | | | |
| Pilates | | | | |
| Rowing | | | | |

| ACTIVITY | I ENJOY | I DO IT OFTEN | I DO IT SOMETIMES | I NEVER DO IT |
|---|---|---|---|---|
| Rugby | | | | |
| Sailing | | | | |
| Singing | | | | |
| Swimming | | | | |
| T'ai Chi | | | | |
| Tennis | | | | |
| Volleyball | | | | |
| Walking | | | | |
| Yoga | | | | |
| Other | | | | |

Even fishing involves some walking and stretching and plenty of fresh air. If you have ticked the first column and then the second, full marks. If there are ticks in the first and then only in the third or fourth, ask yourself 'Why?' What excuses have you got for not doing more of what you enjoy, to enhance your health and fitness?

Gentle stretching will improve the natural blood flow through the muscles, disperse lactic acid and prevent rigidity and hunching. Notice how some elderly people are stooped forward. They have habitually allowed their front shoulder and stomach muscles to contract over the years, and the back muscles to stretch, causing a C shape.

So here are some simple stretches you can practise any time, for just a few seconds, to ensure that you never become out of shape. All stretching exercises should be slow and gentle, so take your time, and only stretch as far as your body lets you without causing pain.

## Seated stretch

Sit comfortably in a firm chair and relax. Drop your shoulders and gently move your right ear towards your right shoulder. Now move the left ear to the left shoulder. Repeat a couple of times. Now turn your head and look to your right. Now left. And repeat. Next gently allow your head to drop down so that your chin moves towards your chest. Hold it for a moment. Feel the stretch in the back of your neck and in your upper back. Drop your shoulders a little more. Gently lift your head back to a central position.

Raise your right arm above your head. Bend the elbow and place your hand on the back of your neck, fingers pointing down towards your lower back. With your left hand gently take hold of your right elbow and pull it back. Feel the stretch in your upper right arm. Hold it for a count of ten, releasing tension in your shoulders. Try not to jut your head forward as you do this exercise. Repeat with your left arm above your head, and your right hand helping it to push back and stretch. Hold it for a count of ten and release.

Now lock your fingers together and raise both arms above your head. Turn the palms out to face the ceiling. Hold for a count of ten. Drop your shoulders. Open your eyes and mouth wide as you count. Exercising your facial muscles will help to maintain a bright, wide-awake look.

Next place your hands on the sides of your waist, thumbs pointing backwards. Pull your shoulders back and take your elbows as if to meet each other. Feel the space between your shoulder blades squeezing and contracting. Arch your back a little and look up at the ceiling, keeping your mouth open as you do this.

To complete your sitting stretch, with your hands still on your waist, turn the upper part of your body, from the waist, and look back over your right shoulder. Only go as far as is comfortable. Count to ten. Return to the centre. Then to the left.

These are simple exercises you can do anywhere, at your desk, on the kitchen stool, when you've been sitting in the car for a long period.

### Standing stretch

First of all, STAND WELL. (See the standing relaxation on page 33.) Gently rock backwards and forwards on the balls and heels of your feet – rather like a policeman ('Evenin' all'). Policemen and soldiers do this to ease the tension on their spines which builds up as they stand for long periods. Feel the stretching and contraction of the calf muscles as you do this slowly. Gradually increase the stretch until you are standing on tiptoe. Relax down again.

Now shrug your shoulders a couple of times. Circle your right shoulder forwards three times, then backwards three times. Don't forget to breathe. Now your left shoulder, forwards . . . and back. Now circle your right arm forwards, taking it above your head and down at the back. Now the left. Circle your right arm backwards, bringing it down at the front. And the left arm. Relax.

Now take both arms above your head and interlace the fingers. Turn the palms of the hands upwards. Drop the shoulders and feel the stretch as you reach upwards. Feel the muscles of your arms stretching. And now slowly bring yourself on to the tips of your toes. Feel that stretch throughout your body, lengthening your back, introducing space between all those compressed organs in your body. Count to ten. Open the arms out wide and begin to bring them down in a wide sweeping circle. Relax your feet gently as your arms travel down to your sides.

## Yoga

Yoga is a wonderful key to relaxation – it's how I was first introduced to it. Gentle stretching and concentration on the postures focuses your mind and calms your body and your emotions. Anyone can take up Yoga, at any age. I often think of the woman in the class who did the splits for the first time when she was 70 years old! It was a wonderful lesson in being as young as you want to be. Yoga is non-competitive, with the emphasis on what *your* body can do and can benefit from. You don't have to be able to get into the lotus position or do the splits to enjoy the relaxing and stilling benefits. There are a number of different approaches to Yoga, some of which concentrate on meditative exercises rather than physical, and there are some which do both. Yoga has the effect of stilling your mind and calming your body, making you more aware of tensions and blockages which prevent you relaxing. Contact your local library for details of classes in your area.

## Massage

Having your face and body massaged by someone else gives you benefits on a number of levels:

- Physically, it helps to relieve muscular tensions and encourage the healthy flow of blood round the body
- Mentally, it can help soothe you and wind you down so that you can regain your sense of perspective
- Emotionally, it gives you a feeling of being pampered, being important and worthwhile, so enhancing your self-esteem.

A session with a professional masseur/masseuse is wonderful of course, but you don't have to pay to go to a masseur. You can practise gentle massage with a partner or friend. Get your partner to sit down on a straight-backed chair, facing away from you. As you stand behind them, begin to stroke their forehead gently, as if smoothing away the worry lines. First of all stroke upwards, starting at the eyebrows, using sweeping movements with the flat of the fingers of each hand. After a few moments, start at the centre of the forehead and sweep outwards. Do this for five or ten minutes, then swap roles. It's very soothing for the stroker and the strokee!

You can massage yourself too. Take your fingers to the back of your neck and cup your neck in your hands. Then, moving only the fingers, gently massage the back of your head and your neck. Gentle circular movements will stimulate the flow of blood and ease tension. Try it a bit further down your neck, working each side of the vertebrae, rather than on the backbone. Relax your hands down again.

Now take hold of the left large shoulder muscle between the fingers and the heel of your right hand and knead them as if you were kneading bread. Gently, but enough to stimulate the flow of blood. Then massage the opposite shoulder in the same way. This is where a lot of tension is stored, particularly if you have a sedentary job.

## Alexander Technique

Look around you as you walk down the street, or as you sit in a public place. Notice how adult people hold their bodies when they are sitting, standing and walking. Many are stooped, with shoulders hunched, backs arched, weight unevenly balanced on one foot, spines contorted and heads thrust forward. Over time, the results of these bad habits are seen in back pain, migraine and numerous other aches and pains as muscles in the body have to take far more strain than they are designed for. This in turn affects our breathing and our mental and emotional state and can lead to a spiral into depression, lack of energy and confidence and general feelings of lethargy and inability to cope.

Then notice how children, particularly those under the age of three-and-a-half, sit, stand, run and bend, breathe, laugh and live with boundless energy. They have a natural, innate ability to conserve energy by using their muscles in the most efficient way and by breathing correctly. Don't we all wonder, from time to time, just where children get all that energy from? That innate ability to hold our bodies in the best way to retain our energy and balance is often lost as we age. The Alexander Technique is a way of helping you to re-educate your body (and mind) and to regain that lost energy and dispel stress and pain. It is a self-help technique; while you need a teacher to put you on the right track, your teacher is helping *you* to become aware of *your own* tensions and physical imbalances so that you can correct them, little by little, day by day, moment to moment.

Frederick Alexander was an Australian actor, born in the 1860s, whose promising career was all but ended when his voice gave out on him. When conventional medicine failed to help him, he decided to take his problems into his own hands and, in so doing, discovered a powerful new way of using his whole body with coordination and balance, thus restoring it to health.

Alexander noticed that when he was acting and reciting, there was excessive muscular tension, principally in his neck and back, causing him to hold his head unnaturally rigidly on his spine. He observed that when his head and neck were tense, the rest of his body followed suit, causing pain and stiffness in the chest, legs and even the feet. After months of experimentation and trial and error, he discovered that by positioning his head correctly on his neck and spine and by releasing the tensions in his neck and back, he was freeing up the muscles of his whole body. This released tension, eased his breathing and enabled him to speak powerfully and clearly with minimum effort. The effect on his whole body and general well-being was positive and life-enhancing.

Since then, many thousands of people have benefited from Alexander Technique. For many it has relieved long-standing and seemingly incurable back problems. For others it has been a preventative measure, providing the means to a more graceful and elegant posture, a lightness and suppleness, where the muscles are used efficiently and without strain. Overall, there comes a greater feeling of well-being, of ease and freedom of movement and peace of mind as students achieve greater awareness of their bodies and the effects on their emotional and mental state, and are able to identify and free tension as soon as it starts.

An important element of the Technique is the ability to pause and think for a few seconds before moving the body or reacting to a stimulus. All animals do this – they get themselves into the position in which their muscles will be used most efficiently, and then they move. As you practise, the pause will become so automatic and natural that it will be almost imperceptible. You will do it as naturally as focusing your eyes. As you progress, your awareness of your body posture will undo those harmful and unconscious habits which cause pain and stress in your body. You will begin automatically to find yourself in the correct position to take the next move, whether sitting, standing, twisting, bending, lifting or resting. Alexander summed it up perfectly when he said, 'If you stop doing the wrong thing, the right thing will emerge naturally.'

My Alexander Technique teacher tells me of the many benefits his students have reported. The most obvious are:

- improved balance and coordination
- better breathing
- increased mental awareness
- ability to be still and calm
- increased awareness of self in space
- using the body economically and efficiently
- increased ability to think in movement
- better ability to undertake tasks step by step.

Throughout all this there is the facility to live moment to moment, developing the 'means whereby' approach rather than the habitual 'end-gaining' attitude to life. Teachers of Alexander Technique undergo extensive training – a three year course of part-time study in a college, together with home study. The Society of Alexander Teachers (STAT) recommends teacher training courses and they have lists of fully qualified teachers in all areas of the country (see Quick Reference 2, page 107 for details).

## Sleep

Getting enough sleep is crucial to keeping stress at bay. A friend who recently had a baby rang me to say she couldn't cope. After six weeks of feeding, changing, getting up at all hours, being unable to have a nap when she wanted, she was desperate. The following week when I went to see her, I prepared myself for a sad sight. When I arrived, she was out in the front garden, watering her flowers, with her make-up on, hair immaculate, looking like a million dollars and feeling great. Why? The baby had started to sleep through much of the night and she was getting some rest. She felt able to cope and was positive and cheerful.

We have a body clock, a biological rhythm which works on a 24-hour pattern. Our sleep hormones prepare us for rest at roughly the same time each evening. If we have an erratic pattern of sleeping, they can be thrown into confusion, so if you can, try to go to bed and get up at about the same times each day. This 'beds in' your natural hormonal rhythms.

Don't assume that if you're not getting seven or eight hours sleep each night there's something wrong. Some people only need five or six hours. Experiments carried out in the US Army have shown that gradual, planned reduction of sleep by one or two hours per night can be handled quite readily, so long as the level remains above five hours. Less than five hours, on a regular basis, can lead to loss of concentration, irritability and a tendency to make mistakes. It is the quality, not the quantity that's important. The test is – do you feel tired the next day?

## Preparation and environment

Wind down gradually for sleep. Don't take vigorous exercise within two hours of your bedtime, as your body will be energised and will resist sleep. Instead, lie on the sofa, watch some TV, read a book, take a shower, and prepare yourself psychologically for sleep.

Avoid eating anything other than a light snack and keep away from coffee and alcohol. Alcohol can induce sleep, but won't provide you with quality rest, and you may wake early and feel tired. Nicotine is a stimulant and will impede healthy sleep.

Most people sleep best when the room temperature is about 60–65 degrees. If you have a street light outside your bedroom invest in some thick, dark curtains. Make sure your room is adequately ventilated. Have a window open, but not one which places you directly in a flow of cold air. Wear ear-plugs if you are a shift worker, or live on a busy road.

## Wear and tear

Sleep helps the body repair itself and so is crucial to good health. Don't worry though if you have missed sleep for a period for good reasons – new baby, death in the family, hectic social life. The body is a wonderful mechanism, and will catch up on itself quickly when you do fall into a more regular sleeping pattern.

## Early morning stress syndrome

Many people I work with report feeling tired at night, going off to sleep as soon as their heads hit the pillow, and then waking at three or four in the morning. They are unable to get back to sleep and often lie there worrying about the past or the future until day mercifully dawns. They may report breaking out in a cold sweat and feeling panicky and alarmed.

Have you had this experience? The harder you try to go to sleep the more anxious you feel and the more sleep escapes you. You lie there telling yourself, 'I've *got* to get to sleep. I've got that big meeting/ visitors/so much to do tomorrow.' All these messages make you more tense and less likely to sleep. What's worse, lying there in the darkness seems to heighten all the normal tensions and worries of the day, and they can build up into huge problems which seem impossible to overcome.

Waking early (and often suddenly) is a very common symptom of stress and one which I've come across a great deal in situations such as job loss, bereavement, marital breakup, financial problems and many others. If this applies to you, try the following:

- Think of it as a normal and natural symptom of stress, one which many people experience and overcome. It isn't pleasant, but it's not going to do you any permanent harm. Remember your body will catch up eventually.
- Get up, switch on a light (downstairs preferably, so that the whole family isn't disturbed), walk about, make a milky drink and read the paper or a book for a while. Putting the light on

and doing something, rather than just lying there tossing and turning, can help to calm you down and restore you to a more balanced frame of mind. Explain to your partner why you may need to do this, so that they don't feel too disturbed or worried by your disappearance.

· When you go back to bed, mentally go through your favourite relaxation routine (see above). Let your muscles relax and flop heavily into the mattress. Concentrate on allowing the tension to flow out of your body, particularly in those areas where you know you hold tension. A neighbour who attended home relaxation sessions with me discovered for the first time that she was in the habit of keeping her jaw clenched and her teeth gritted together as she went to sleep and when she awoke. She concentrated on allowing a feeling of heaviness and softness to flow into her jaw and found she slept much better. Often it will be your face that holds the most tension as you try to sleep – your forehead, your eyes, your jaw. Go through a mental checklist. Feel:
  · your forehead becoming higher and wider
  · the space between your eyes increasing
  · your eye sockets deepening
  · your cheeks flopping loosely towards the pillow
  · your jaw becoming soft and warm
  · your lips parting gently
  · your temples releasing tension and allowing space
  · the back of your head and neck giving in to the pillow.
· Then visit your mental refuge. Imagine yourself in a place you would most like to be – on the golf course, lying on a beach, walking through a wood, in a cottage, looking out over a beautiful landscape – whatever makes you feel happy and relaxed. Bring to mind all the details of that experience. Who is there with you? Are you alone? What are the sights, the colours, the smells, the sounds, the feelings?

If you suffer from chronic insomnia and it has persisted for a very long time, see your doctor. Sleeping pills, while not the answer for extended periods, can help you to catch up on your sleep, for example during a particularly difficult period of your life. When you are back on an even keel, then you can dispense with them.

## Laughter therapy

Humour is becoming a recognised way of dealing with anxiety. It does more than just exercise your internal organs – though that in itself does you a power of good. Having a good laugh releases into your body the same hormones (endorphins) that are released when you take brisk exercise. They make you feel good, and put you on a 'high'. Surprising as it may seem, they even work when you smile. So watch an episode of your favourite TV series or have a laugh with a friend when you're feeling down. An American cancer sufferer, diagnosed terminally ill, claims to have cured himself and amazed his doctors simply by watching scores of side-splitting tapes from his hospital bed.

> *No man is a failure who is enjoying life*
> William Feather, author, 1889–1981

Laugh at yourself. So you make mistakes and look foolish sometimes. Who doesn't? Join the rest of the human race. Make a joke of your shortcomings and you make friends with yourself and with others. People who smile and laugh tend to attract others who do the same. They have a generally positive effect on the people they associate with. You could be changing the lives of a few other people, as well as your own!

## The Mask of the King

Long ago there was a wicked king who ruled a land which was torn apart by strife. His life was in constant danger from his subjects who hated his harshness and cruelty. Realising how deeply unhappy his life was, he sent for his wizard.

'What can I do', he said, 'to change myself?'

The wizard thought for a moment and said, 'I can help you, but you must do exactly as I say.'

'Anything,' the king replied, 'which will make me happier and give me peace of mind.'

The wizard went away and when he returned he held in his hand a mask which was a likeness of the king. Unlike the face of the king, however, which was lined with frowns and dark as thunder, the mask showed a bright and smiling face. The wizard asked the king to put it on, and to wear it always.

'I can't wear that!' said the king, 'it isn't anything like me and how I really feel.'

'Put it on,' said the wizard, 'or I can't help you.'

The king put on the mask and wore it everywhere he went. As he travelled round his kingdom, he was amazed at how people responded to him. His subjects smiled and waved at him. Pleased with their friendliness, the king began to treat them with respect and consideration. They grew to trust and love him. Very soon the strife which had been widespread throughout the country got less and less until it disappeared altogether.

But still the king was dissatisfied. Though everything else had changed, he knew that he was only wearing a mask, and he felt like a fraud. He sent for the wizard again.

'Now my kingdom is at peace,' he said, 'but I cannot continue to deceive my people. I must remove the mask.'

'Very well,' said the wizard.

With beating heart, and eyes tightly closed, the king stood in front of his mirror and fearfully removed the mask which had transformed his life. Plucking up all his courage, he opened his eyes to look at the frowning face which he had covered up all this time.

What he saw amazed and delighted him. By some miracle, his own face had changed beyond recognition. His eyes sparkled, his brow was smooth and wrinkle-free and his smile radiated throughout the room. The inner changes which the mask had brought him were now shown brightly on his face.

## You are what you eat

A wholesome and healthy diet can help you to increase your resistance to stress. Yet it's usually when you are most stressed that your diet most suffers. When you're rushed you snatch processed junk meals containing high amounts of fat and sugar, just to fill you up and keep you going.

- It's well publicised these days that saturated fats raise cholesterol levels. The foods which are high in saturated fat are butter, cream, cheese, palm and coconut oils. High amounts of cholesterol are found in egg yolk, meat and prawns.
- Cut down your sugar and salt intake. Salt can cause high blood pressure. Look at processed foods carefully and see how they are made up. There are surprisingly large amounts of sugar and salt, added, so it is said, to please the Western palate. You can re-educate your palate not to want so much of these items.
- Prune down your coffee intake. Caffeine has a temporary stimulating effect, but it soon wears off and leaves you craving for more.
- You don't have to cut out alcohol altogether, but be aware of your intake. If you like alcohol, one or two moderately sized drinks per day is sensible, unless your doctor advises against it. Drink plenty of water – eight glasses a day is ideal.
- Eat more fish. The instance of heart disease in Japan is a small

fraction of that in Western countries. The Japanese diet is high in fish, rice and green vegetables, low in fats and dairy products.

- Eat more fibre. Fibre is filling and satisfying and aids elimination of waste products.
- We are told to eat well at breakfast, less at lunch and less again in the evenings. While this is sensible advice, it doesn't always fit our work, social and family patterns very well. It's better, as you eat, to be aware of your body's real needs. Think: 'What do I really need right now, to make me feel satisfied and to leave me alert and feeling healthy?' And make a habit of stopping eating before you are full to bursting, even if it means not clearing your plate. Avoid late meals as this may upset your sleep patterns and will interfere with the body's natural cycle of processing and eliminating food. Upsetting this cycle can cause inefficient digestion and can lead to weight gain.

## Smoking

Smoking can cause premature aging of the skin, especially the face. While you may feel that smoking eases your tension, some of that pleasing effect is being given by the long slow breaths you take when you inhale. Try the breathing without the smoking. The potentially harmful effects of smoking are well-publicised. Nicotine causes constriction of the blood flow and this hampers rather than aids relaxation.

## My lifestyle

Complete the following questionnaire to tell you more about how your lifestyle might be affecting your stress levels and therefore your ability to relax.

Score 3 points for true, 2 for partly true, 1 for untrue.

|  | TRUE | PARTLY TRUE | UNTRUE |
|---|---|---|---|
| 1. I exercise two or three times per week for at least 20 minutes | | | |
| 2. I have a healthy diet which includes fibre, fresh fruit and vegetables | | | |
| 3. I do not smoke | | | |
| 4. I drink alcohol in moderation (two drinks per day) or not at all | | | |
| 5. Whenever possible I walk, rather than drive/ride in transport | | | |
| 6. I take meals at regular times and I allow time to digest them | | | |
| 7. I put aside time each week for my hobbies and interests | | | |
| 8. I get enough sleep for my needs | | | |
| 9. I spend some time outside each day | | | |
| 10. I have a holiday each year | | | |

If you have scored between 10 and 19 you need to readjust your lifestyle significantly, in order to feel more relaxed. If you have scored between 20 and 24 you're doing some things well. But there's room for improvement. If you have scored between 25 and 30 your healthy lifestyle will help you deal with stress. Don't rest on your laurels!

# 6 Change your mind – change your body

When you release mental and emotional pressure on yourself, your body responds by becoming healthier. You might immediately feel taller, lighter, straighter, more supple. Your breathing patterns will change. Stress-related illnesses won't get a look-in.

Because of the loop between your mind and your body, your fitness and health reinforce a state of mental well-being and happiness. So this chapter deals with various ways in which you can achieve greater mental health. You'll want to celebrate that achievement!

## Positive affirmations

The mind influences the body and the body influences the mind. Each has an immensely powerful effect on the other. We've already talked about how your physical tensions and pain can make you feel lethargic, helpless and depressed, causing the vicious circle, or stress spiral, to send you further and further down. There are many ways of breaking into the vicious circle – giving yourself positive messages or affirmations is one of them. Every action is preceeded by a thought. Your thoughts create your experiences.

To affirm means to make firm something which you are saying to yourself. By practising positive affirmations they become part of your life, and they become real. Our subconscious mind is like that part of a huge iceberg which is submerged under water. It is very non-judgemental. It believes what we tell it. Then it affects very directly how we feel. We all experience feelings of depression and elation, for what we think is no apparent reason. This is our subconscious mind giving us feedback from the dozens and dozens of pieces of information which we give it every day. So if your daily round consists of you telling yourself you're useless at sports, hopeless at communicating with people, not attractive, less able than the next person, always nervous about facing up to a new situation, frightened of spiders, then your subconscious mind takes all that on board and sends it back to you in messages about your uselessness and lack of value.

Then, no matter how often others tell us that we look good today, or they like the way we just handled that difficult situation, we deny it, or shrug it off as a dishonest comment, because our subconscious is stuffed full of material which contradicts flattering comments. Your subconscious affects not only your mental state, but your emotional and physical state as well. You set up a negative loop which you may not even be aware of!

Imagine how refreshing it is for the subconscious to receive some positive, encouraging messages! Even if you're not quite sure they're true in the first instance. Your non-judgemental mind accepts these too as the truth and sends back positive messages which directly affect your mind, your emotions and your body.

> *To love oneself is the beginning of a life-long romance*
> Oscar Wilde, author, 1854–1900

Healthcare workers have observed time and time again that the thoughts and feelings of a patient can affect the course of the illness quite remarkably. Negative thoughts and feelings of helplessness and hopelessness appear to hamper the road back to well-being.

If you feel mentally or physically under par, or just want to feel even better than you do now, start a daily routine of standing in front of the mirror (as you shave or put on your make-up) smiling and saying out loud to yourself, 'Every day and in every way, I am getting better and better.' With such positive affirmations repeated daily, your mind and body will respond on a subconscious level to the messages you are giving them. If you're not sure whether they will work, keep repeating them anyway. You've nothing to lose and a lot to gain! Positive affirmations have worked for many thousands of people. If you prefer other sorts of messages, then look at the list of suggestions below. Or buy a CD to play in the car, or at home. When you're faced with difficult problems, periods of self-doubt and stressful situations, spend a few minutes each day giving yourself some positive affirmations to boost up your subconscious powers to work for you. Some positive affirmations which might work for you:

- I am a wonderful and valuable person
- I help other people just by being myself
- I deserve the very best
- I can overcome my pain and be well again
- I am healthy and fit
- I release my past. It has no control over me
- I love and appreciate myself
- The world is a beautiful place
- I let go of all my guilt and fears
- I am relaxed and peaceful
- I have a right to do what I want to do
- I have lots of energy
- I am taking time for myself
- I am a powerful and creative person
- I have a lot to offer
- I love others and they love me
- I am surrounded by loving, healing energies
- I am unique.

If none of these are exactly what you want, substitute a positive affirmation which will be the most powerful and personal to you. Say it out loud several times a day. Meditate on it as you fall asleep. Write it down, and have it by you, in the car, in the kitchen, in the bathroom, in the drawer, on the wall. You don't have to understand why this will work, just keep practising, and you will see the benefits through the whole of your life.

To help you focus on the positive aspects of you, make a list of five things you're very good at, five things that people say you're able to do and five things you *can* do.

YOU CAN complete it. Keep going until it's finished. Which do you think is the most important? Write that one down on a big sheet of paper – make a colourful poster of it and stick it on your wall, your fridge door – or somewhere else where you'll see it constantly.

Add some more positives to your list tomorrow and keep reviewing it regularly, adding even more.

## Positive and negative thinking – is the glass half-empty or half-full?

Your thought processes involve you in constant internal dialogue with yourself. Be aware when you are giving yourself negative feedback. It's like the jiggling fingers telling the brain that all is not well. If you keep feeding your brain with negative information about yourself, you'll feel inadequate, intimidated and impotent. Try this: every time you become aware you are telling yourself – silently or out loud – that you can't do something, or something won't work, give yourself an alternative, positive message. Here are some examples:

| NEGATIVE | POSITIVE |
|---|---|
| I've never been any good at tennis/figures/public speaking | If others can do it, so can I |
| This idea will never work | People have tried more unusual ideas, and they've worked. My idea is a good one |
| I haven't got time for all this relaxation stuff | I can make some time – just a little each day and it will make a difference |

| NEGATIVE | POSITIVE |
|---|---|
| Nobody will want to listen to me | I have some interesting things to say which will benefit others |
| It's bound to rain if we go walking | It'll probably be a lovely day – if it rains we'll enjoy it anyway |
| I can't get on with her at all | If I try to find out more about what makes her tick, I'll discover some points of common interest |
| Nothing ever goes right for me | I have a lot of positive things to celebrate |

If you change the message each time to a positive one, it will start to come naturally, without effort. So that every time anything goes wrong with your life, you're able to put it into perspective among the good things that are happening around you.

> *If you think you can, or if you think you can't, you're right'*
> Henry Ford, founder of the Ford Motor Company,
> 1863–1947

What are your negative thoughts? What can you replace them with?

World class sportsmen often hum or sing so that they can't hear the negative internal voice which comes between them and success!


## Your 'shoulds'

There's a study of the psychology of human behaviour known as Transactional Analysis. It was introduced by an American psychiatrist called Eric Berne, in the 1960s. Among other things it identifies a group of elements which set patterns in our lives at a very early age. Berne calls these patterns 'drivers' or 'scripts' – the messages and motivators which lead or drive us to behave in certain ways so that we'll feel 'OK' about ourselves. These patterns are learned in childhood to help us deal with life then. All too often, we carry them with us into our adulthood, when they've outlived their usefulness. These drivers make us do, think and feel things which are no longer appropriate – yet we can't seem to shake them off. This is because we often don't get as far as identifying, or becoming aware of them, in the first place.

In my coaching work with stressed people in industry and commerce, I often hear my clients say: 'For some reason, I feel I should do everything 110%, to the best of my ability, and this gives me real problems, because there simply isn't time'; or 'I have to keep driving myself harder and harder, I can't seem to stop'; or 'Naturally I should think of everyone else's needs before mine – it's selfish otherwise, isn't it?'

Berne identified five main drivers which become established when we are children. Some people have all of them, some just one or two. People can feel that they are not OK unless they are acting them out.

## 1. Be perfect

This can make you feel that you always have to excel, or get things completely right. 'Fit for purpose' isn't good enough, it has to be a 'Rolls-Royce' job. Anything less than perfection is failure, and mistakes are major traumas. For those in work, it becomes difficult to delegate, since you cannot trust anyone else to work to your perfectionist standards. You'd rather do it yourself than risk a less than excellent job and those mere mortals who work for you know it. This is, in fact, an excellent way to constantly beat yourself up and give yourself (and others) stress.

*The stressful script* – I'm not OK unless I do everything perfectly.

*The relaxing script* – It's OK to be good enough, and to make things fit for purpose.

## 2. Be strong

Being strong is an admirable driver which leads you to be fiercely independent, self-sufficient and undemanding of others. It's standing on your own two feet. However, the down-side is that you can find it difficult to express emotion and to seek help when you really need it. People probably won't even realise that you need support, as you always appear to cope so well, and are probably the one who *gives* support to others most of the time. Again delegation may be difficult, since it implies inability to cope. And dealing with a profoundly sad event may be doubly difficult if you cannot share your feelings with anyone.

*The stressful script* – I have to manage on my own, or I am showing weakness.

*The relaxing script* – It's OK to ask for help and to show my feelings.

## 3. Try harder

This often leads you to try things which do not really interest you, simply because your driver tells you that you should at least have a go. The trying can become the end, rather than the means to an end. So you may find that you stick doggedly to a lost cause, because giving up would seem like failure. Often achieving does not bring a feeling of success, as it may set up expectations in others that you will try even harder. You may find yourself spending a lot of time doing things which do not interest you, to the detriment of things which you find exciting and fulfilling. This inability to discriminate and take control can be very stressful.

*The stressful script* – I must have a go at everything and I must not give up.

*The relaxing script* – It's OK to achieve something and it's OK not to try to do things which don't interest me.

## 4. Hurry up

Many people feel that if their days are not packed full of action from dawn till dusk, they are not doing enough. 'Work, work and never cease to work' was the Victorian ethic. 'You'll get plenty of rest and sleep after you're dead.' If you are not mentally and physically exhausted by the end of the day, then you could have done more. Our culture is a *do* culture, and not a *be* culture. And yet we are human beings, not human doings. If you are driven by this pattern, you might constantly plan your next move, show impatience with others' slowness, anticipate what they're going to say and hustle them into acting more quickly than they feel comfortable with. It's likely that you will be unable to just sit and watch TV or read a book in the garden as you will spot tidying or weeding which needs to be done.

*The stressful script* – I must get through as much as possible and then some more.

*The relaxing script* – It's OK for me and others to take things slowly and to just BE sometimes.

## 5. Please people

This is a very common driver. We are brought up to believe that we must put the needs of others before our own, or we will be selfish. Yet you cannot help anyone if you are stressed out and unable to cope with the demands which others put on you. You might even go out of your way to please people you don't even know – 'What will the people in the bus queue think?' 'I'd better not complain to the shop assistant – she'll think badly of me.' Pleasing others all the time means that you lose track of what pleases you and, in this way, you are giving yourself a lifelong message that you don't matter, your wishes and views are of no value.

*The stressful script* – Other people's needs must always come before mine.

*The relaxing script* – It's OK to please myself as well as others, even if it sometimes means I have to say NO.

Pause for a moment to reflect. Which are the two drivers that best describe you? How do they contribute to your stress levels?

Drivers are not wrong – they may be very useful to you in many circumstances. Be aware when they are not and live your life to a more suitable and relevant script.

# Letting go of the past

Your emotional baggage about what has happened in the past may be a source of constant stress. It isn't easy to let go of feelings of anger and resentment against others who have injured and hurt you. And yet these feelings are often far more destructive to you than they are for the person who should be at the receiving end. You can choose whether you allow that to have power over you now. Ask yourself: 'Am I going to let that person/event poison my life, spoil my happiness?' 'Am I going to let them have that much power over me?' Or 'I'll demonstrate, by my calm and mature behaviour, that there is more in my life than worrying about them.'

Make a mental image of a past event which still upsets you. Imagine circus music playing as you look at the scene. Transform it into a lighter event. Some of my business colleagues who have had to suffer a pompous or intimidating person at work make a habit of imagining that person on the toilet. Try it with someone who has overpowered you. You can use your creativity to put a past or present event in perspective by introducing any light-hearted or ridiculous element of your choice.

Sometimes you need to forgive yourself as well as others for things which have happened in the past. Which of us can honestly say we haven't experienced a number of things we need to give and receive forgiveness for? Leave them in the past where they belong.

# Stop/start

'I must stop getting so worried about my workload.'
'I wish I could stop getting angry with Jim.'
'I've got to stop eating so much and get rid of this flab.'

These phrases might actually stop you from moving forward, as they are constantly reminding you of a situation or circumstance you want to *move away from*.

Replace them with positive thoughts of what you can *move towards*. The brain can't negate. Focus on what you want and what pleases you.

Move *towards* that goal and the baggage of the past will naturally fall away.

'I will organise my work better so that I have more time.'

'I will practise my breathing exercises when I meet Jim.'

'Look out for the new, slim me, after this diet.'

## You're in charge

When people get you down, it may be because you are *giving them the power* to hassle and worry you. Some of those people really don't deserve so much power. You have choices. Ask yourself: 'Am I going to allow this person to affect me like this? Or will I choose to take that power away from them, by doing what I believe is right and not worrying about what they think?'

## Living in the present

Eastern philosophies lay much greater emphasis than Western beliefs on the importance of the present. *'Be here now'* is a helpful phrase to repeat to yourself when you get caught up in the stress of anticipation. Look around you and really notice all the things which you can appreciate in the present. Western lives are very wrapped up in thoughts of the future and it is only when we go for a long stroll in the country or pause to watch a sunset that we realise how much of life passes us by unnoticed. When you catch yourself stewing about what might or might not go wrong in the future, remind yourself to 'Be Here Now'. Things often work out surprisingly differently from the way you expect, and all that time you spend worrying is usually completely wasted.

### Parking zone

A useful way to allow yourself to be in the present is to 'park' your worries, and promise yourself that you will come back to them another time, in a week, a month or a year. 'I'll really let myself worry about that one on 22 June.' This technique works wonderfully well when you are trying to remember someone's name too. Park it, or put it on a shelf, leave it in your unconscious and often it pops up sorted!

> *I'll think of it all tomorrow . . . After all, tomorrow is*
> *another day*
> Scarlett O'Hara, heroine, *Gone with the Wind*, 1936

# 7 Your 'resourceful state'

Your resources are your natural strengths. Being stressed means feeling, thinking and *being* unresourceful. You don't feel you have what it takes to cope with the situation. You might feel that someone else is taking your resources away from you – for example, when someone intimidates or frightens you. Or it may be that the circumstances you are in present huge problems, and you feel your resources are small and insignificant – like David facing Goliath.

If you believe you can't do it, then you won't. So how can you change that around into believing in yourself? How can you tap into the natural resources which you undoubtedly have and build on them?

Try this. As you sit/lie/stand there right now, think of a time when you felt really strong and resourceful. Think of the specific situation you were in at the time. You were feeling positive, energised, 'on a roll'. The things you wanted were happening for you. You knew you were doing well and you felt you could move mountains. It can be any situation at all, work, home, social, on holiday, in the bath . . . whenever. It could be a feeling you had for days or months, or it could be a feeling you had just for a moment.

Because you now need to concentrate on your inner self, and not on the written page, you'll need to read this through before you can begin. Alternatively, get someone to read it out to you, allowing you plenty of time between each sentence for you to carry out the suggestion.

## Stage I

*Visualise*

Close your eyes and 'get into' that situation. What mental images come into your mind? Have you a picture of what was happening? What sort of picture? Is it small or large? Black and white or coloured? Are you *in* the scene, or are you an observer, watching yourself in the scene? Is the picture still or moving?

*Listen*

Notice what sounds you're hearing. Are there voices? Your own voice? Speaking to others? To yourself? What internal messages are you giving yourself in this situation? What other sounds are there?

*Feel*

Concentrate on the feelings you have. What are they? Excitement? Happiness? Contentment? Strength? Something else? Where do you feel that physically within yourself? Pinpoint where that is and hold your concentration on it.

## Stage 2

*Anchor yourself*

Pinch your right ear gently between your fingers and maintain this through the next stage. (Read on! All will be revealed.)

## Stage 3

*Visualise*

Revisit your mental picture. Make it bigger. Maybe so big that it surrounds you. If it's black and white, start colouring it in. Let the colours get brighter and brighter. Introduce movement. The picture becomes more and more vivid. If you are an observer, become a part of that picture, so that you are in it yourself, a part of that vital, colourful scene. What else do you want to do to make the picture more intense? . . . Increase the pressure a little on your ear.

*Listen*

Now the sound. Make it louder. Make it more attractive in whatever way you like. Introduce music, or make the sound sweeter in a way which pleases you. Allow that to grow until it's enough for you . . . Increase the pressure a little more on your ear.

*Feel*

Revisit the feeling. Make it increase in intensity. Feel the physical effects as you allow this to happen. Take your time. Don't stop until you've let the feeling grow as much as you want it to. Really enjoy the feeling of resourcefulness and ability to manage yourself which this gives you . . . Increase the pressure on your ear.

You have now tapped into your own resourceful state. Unpinch your ear. Relax, look around you, have a stretch. Now repeat stages 2 and 3 as often as you like until you feel you've really got it, until the process has 'bedded in'. Some people find it easier than others to find mental pictures, or sounds or feelings, so don't worry if you can't access all three. Keep working on the ones you can access.

Next time you feel unresourceful, pinch your right ear and the process will start up automatically. You have programmed it into your brain and it will re-run. That resourcefulness will help you get through your current situation successfully.

Pinching your ear is only one example of an *anchor* which will help you access your desired state. It could equally be carrying a lucky rabbit's foot, or wearing a particular item of clothing. Whatever it is, when you have that, you re-run your programme of resourcefulness.

## Detach yourself

Part of your resourcefulness is your ability to relax by stepping out of the difficult situation you're in and looking at it in a detached, dissociated way. Think of a situation which has caused you stress and anxiety. Make a mental image of that event. What can you see in that place? What sounds? Smells? Where are you in this picture? What else do you notice about the image? How do you feel as you recapture the scene?

Imagine that someone has photographed the event. Now you are wandering around a picture gallery looking at a black and white photo of it. You are an objective viewer, looking in from outside. What is going on? What does it look, sound and feel like from that perspective? Notice how you have distanced yourself from the hurtful emotions and the anxiety. Practise until it becomes automatic.

# 8 Be assertive

Louise found it impossible to relax. She was always harassed and seemed to spend her life rushing round doing things for her family and friends. When she was invited out, or asked for help, she would always agree to go, even if she didn't want to or felt too tired, because people expected that of her. 'Why don't people realise,' she said, 'that I have a demanding full-time job, and I need to be able to rest and put my feet up in the evenings sometimes?' 'Do you ever tell them?' I asked. 'Well no, *they should know.*'

## Decide what you want and let others know

The fact is, people don't *know* if you don't tell them. And sometimes you have to tell them things they don't want to hear. Being assertive is recognising and acknowledging the needs of others, but looking after your own needs and rights by explaining clearly what *you* want. This isn't always easy, particularly if you have always fallen in with other people's ideas for you. But it's about you making some choices about how *you* want to spend your life, and telling others clearly about your decisions. Sometimes this means saying *no,* and sticking to it.

> *When choosing between two evils, I always like to try the one I've never tried before*
> Mae West, Hollywood star, 1892–1980

Being assertive is all about respecting yourself and being honest, with yourself and with others. Assertiveness is necessary for your well-being; it raises and maintains your self-esteem and it applies just as much to your treatment of demanding family members or friends, as it does to dealing with unhelpful shop assistants.

It's useful to think of our reactions in three categories – *Passive, Aggressive and Assertive*. We choose to react in these ways to demands which are placed upon us and our reaction can determine how much stress and anxiety we feel afterwards.

So, for example, if Louise continues to be passive, she will carry on bending to other people's requirements, while they may be blissfully unaware of the stress she is feeling. Her stress levels will rocket, as she feels less and less able to control her life. She will continue to feel harassed and bad about her inability to organise her life properly.

If, on the other hand, she lets it build up until she eventually blows a fuse, someone who's least expecting it, and probably least deserving of it, will get an aggressive explosion of pent-up emotions which may destroy a valued relationship. The likelihood is that she will then feel guilty and remorseful and wish she had handled it better. Her stress levels will still be high.

If she respects her own needs, asserts her rights to choose what to do with her evenings and is open and honest with her friends, then her stress levels will drop. She will find herself saying *no* sometimes. Her friends may see her less often, but when she's with them she will really enjoy it and want to be there. Everyone will benefit from her more relaxed state. She will feel in control and therefore good about herself and about her ability to manage her life well.

If you ask around, you'll find that friends and colleagues have a high regard for people who are able to be clear and assertive about their needs. In a family situation it's often more blurred and less easy, and there can certainly be more emotional blackmail – 'You can't really love me if you won't do this for me . . .' It still applies even though it's not easy, and it will, in the long run, help you to feel more relaxed.

## How assertive are you?

Put yourself in the following situations and decide how you typically react. Put a ring round a, b or c.

1. A friend borrowed £20 from you several weeks ago. Clearly she has forgotten. Do you:
   a. Fume inwardly but not mention it?
   b. Remind her about the loan and say that you now need to be repaid?
   c. Fall out with her since she obviously doesn't consider your feelings?

2. You've had a hard day, and you're looking forward to putting your feet up and settling down quietly with a good book. Your neighbour drops in and insists that what you *really* need is to get changed, have a shower, go out ten-pin bowling with him and then on to the 'Rajah' for a curry. Do you:
   a. Tell him you don't need his advice and ask him to leave?
   b. Sigh, get changed and go to the bowling alley with him?
   c. Thank him for his suggestion but say, 'No, not tonight, I have other plans'?

3. You need help in a shop, but the two assistants are busy chatting about their holidays. Do you:
   a. Hide behind the shelves and hope they'll finish their conversation soon?
   b. Remind them that customers pay their wages and demand attention loudly?
   c. Calmly say, 'I'd like some help finding what I need'?

4. You're sitting in your garden on a sunny day and the neighbour is playing loud jazz music next door. You don't like jazz and you were hoping for some peace and quiet. Do you:
   a. Ask the neighbour if he would turn the sound down to an acceptable level?
   b. Put cotton wool in your ears?
   c. Put on your loudest rock record at full volume?

5. You've planned a weekend away for yourself and the family. The neighbour asks you if you can take their son Richard along, to give her a break. Neither you nor your children like Richard very much. Do you:
   a. Agree to take him and ask the children to make allowances?
   b. Tell your neighbour you're fed up with being taken advantage of, and anyway the children don't get on?
   c. Explain that this particular weekend is an important family time and that you won't be taking anyone else along.

6. The boss asks you if you can work late tonight to catch up with an unexpected order. It is your daughter's school concert and she is looking forward to your attending. Do you:
   a. Tell the boss he's already had his pound of flesh and it's typical of him to spring things on you at the last minute?
   b. Tell the boss you are not able to stay tonight, but suggest that you come in a little earlier tomorrow, if the job's that important?
   c. Ring home and apologise to your daughter for not being able to make the concert?

7. A colleague of the opposite sex consistently makes sexual remarks and innuendos. You don't like it. Do you:
   a. Tell them which remarks cause you offence and ask them to stop?
   b. Avoid them whenever possible, and pretend to think the remarks are funny when you can't avoid the person?
   c Shout very loudly at them in public that they are a pervert or a sex maniac?

Answers la, 2b, 3a, 4b, 5a, 6c and 7b are *Passive* reactions.
Answers lc, 2a, 3b, 4c, 5b, 6a and 7c are *Aggressive* reactions.
Answers lb, 2c, 3c, 4a, 5c, 6b and 7a are *Assertive* reactions.

On which reaction – *Passive, Aggressive, Assertive* – did you score most highly? Maybe you scored a mixture, showing that in different situations you demonstrate different reactions. Which situations do you tend to behave assertively in? Jot them down on a piece of paper.

I behave passively in situations when . . .

I behave aggressively in situations when  . . .

I behave assertively in situations when . . .

Think of the tone of your voice. Do you hear yourself barking out commands? Or sounding timid and hesitant? Do you sometimes sound rude and abrupt? Or do you finish your sentences with a question, as if constantly seeking approval?

How do you make the transition from passive or aggressive to assertive?

Take three simple steps:

- *Acknowledge that the other person has a point of view, or a need.*
- *Say what you feel and think, quietly and firmly.*
- *Say what you want to happen. Be quite specific.*

For example:

'I know that you would like me to visit you every week. I feel that will be very difficult with my family commitments. What I'd like to do is to come and see you every other Thursday evening. Then I'd feel relaxed and less hurried.'

'I understand that you need someone to help with the fundraising. I'm really not able to help you right now but I'll certainly ring you if I find that I have some time later in the month.'

## Excuses and justifications

Being assertive means being open, honest and straightforward – you don't have to tie yourself in knots thinking of excuses or fabricating reasons. You don't have to justify or explain away your needs. Your real reasons are good enough. State them firmly and confidently. If someone argues and cajoles, simply restate your needs, firmly and pleasantly, recognising the other point of view, but sticking with your own decision.

Avoid the following – 'Er, I'm sorry to bring it up . . . I hope you don't mind my asking . . . the £20 I lent you . . . I wouldn't normally mind you having it for a bit longer, only I've just been landed with a huge bill and I need it, so I'm really sorry to ask . . .' Sometimes you have to choose between being liked and being respected.

## Ask for time

How many times have you been put on the spot by someone asking you to do something for them, and you've agreed, knowing that it isn't what you want to do? This happens on the telephone, at work and at home. You feel pressured and you agree, then regret it later. 'I wish I hadn't . . .' If you recognise this as one of your stressors, you can do something about it. Whenever you feel disadvantaged in this way, ask for 'thinking it over' time. No matter what the request or the situation, you have a right to organise your thoughts and think about the implications of acting before you agree. You might need to discuss it with a partner, friend or colleague. So a straightforward 'I need to think about it – I'll give you my decision on Tuesday/after lunch/when I've talked to Fred' is fine. This way you are getting back the control you need to make you feel happy about any decision you take. Even if you ask for just five minutes thinking time, it helps.

## Change your mind

You have a right to change your mind, even if you have already set off on one course of action. We can all see more clearly as we get more information or recognise more of the implications. It isn't necessary to stick it out to the bitter end if you're uncomfortable. People may be disappointed – this is the risk you take. You are human, and it's allowed.

## Set clear boundaries

Let people know how far you are prepared to go.

- 'I'll visit you for an hour each Thursday'
- 'I make a point of never lending money'
- 'I need a day to think about this'
- 'I must have an evening free for aerobics once a week'
- 'I am not prepared to interfere in this problem'
- 'I really don't want you to use my
  comb/computer/car/house/idea.'

## Breathing

Use your breathing exercises to calm you and give you confidence before
you assert yourself in a difficult situation. Practise your Emergency Stop
Breath if you're very anxious (see page 30). In any case, fill your lungs
slowly and gently, pause for a moment, then exhale, slowly and in a
controlled way. Repeat this a few times to relax and stabilise you.

## And now . . .

Think back to the beginning of the chapter, and to Louise, my harassed
friend. All that stress because she didn't state her needs assertively. What
stresses do you put on yourself because of non-assertive behaviour?

## Assertiveness checklist

When you're gearing yourself up to behave assertively in a situation you might find it helpful to prepare yourself by reminding yourself of the following points:

1. I am a valuable person, with rights

2. I have a responsibility for myself and to myself

3. I may state clearly what I think and want

4. I may give myself praise for achievements

5. I may make mistakes

6. I may ask for time to make decisions

7. I may change my mind

8. I may state clearly what I am and am not prepared to do

9. I recognise that other people have rights.

# 9 Use others for support

Studies in the USA have shown that cancer is more common in people who bottle up their emotions and try to sort all their problems out for themselves. Being self-sufficient is an admirable quality, but it shouldn't be taken to extremes.

## Informal help and support

We all know about the British stiff upper lip. It's world renowned and we're proud of it. Suppressing feelings and keeping our problems to ourselves is an art form in the UK. We do it magnificently, to Olympic standards. It is also counterproductive and very destructive. Stewing alone about a problem increases your stress levels and keeps the body's alarm button pressed. Letting someone else know how you feel – someone you can trust – lets the pressure out of your system, just like lifting the lid off the pressure cooker. Regular and healthy escapes of steam keep you in balance and better able to handle the demands placed on you.

Close your eyes and think for a moment about people you have talked to, or would consider talking to, about your worries. It may be different people for different problems. Make a list of who they are. Chances are, their qualities include some of the following: trust, confidentiality, discretion, absence of 'judging', empathy, honesty, openness, realism, sense of humour, wisdom, perspective, maturity, genuineness, sincerity, unshockability, good listener.

If you know people who have these qualities, whether they are close family members, neighbours, friends or acquaintances, or in some formal role (doctor or church minister, for example) they may be able to help you through difficult patches. Sometimes even quite a short discussion can help you put worrying things back into perspective and help you take back control of your life.

Think of a problem you have right now. Or some situation which is upsetting you. Or maybe it's a general feeling that you're not performing very well. Who can you talk to about it? Who can you identify with the qualities which are important to you? Ask for their support, for a few minutes of their time. They may not be able to think of a solution, or wave a magic wand to make your problem disappear, but they'll probably be able to help you put it into perspective. If you are worried about burdening them, tell them you don't expect a miracle cure, just a friendly chat. Jot down what's bothering you now, and who you can talk to about it.

Maybe *you* possess a number of these qualities and could provide mutual support for a friend or a colleague, so that you both have someone to turn to in a crisis or difficulty. You are less likely to feel you are burdening someone with your worries if the support is two-way. Remember, you don't have to solve someone else's problem for them, just be there and listen.

If you are not in the habit of disclosing anything about yourself, it may be difficult to start with. Share something not too personal and intimate with someone you can trust and see how it helps. Then gradually you may feel like confiding a little more, when you really need to.

## Professional help and support

1985 was the year of the Manchester Airport disaster. One of my friends survived the experience and soon became aware that there was little or no counselling help and support for survivors of this and many other traumatic events. Nowadays, it is a very different picture. There are a large number of support agencies which you can tap into for telephone or face-to-face help, for general anxiety and stress as well as specific areas of concern, such as traumatic incidents, HIV, child abuse, violence in the family, relationship problems, and many more. Your local GP practise may also be able to offer counselling support to help you through difficulties. In the Quick Reference section on page 107 you'll find a list of some support agencies. It is not comprehensive – you'll find many more, together with local telephone numbers, through your local library, Citizen's Advice Bureau, telephone book and Yellow Pages. It does give some idea of the wide choice of support that's available right now.

## Individual face-to-face counselling and therapy

Alternatively you can talk to a professional counsellor or therapist, a number of whom will be practising in your area. In an agreed number of sessions, for which you pay a fee, you can explore, in complete confidentiality, any areas of your life you want to work on, from increasing your self-esteem, to bereavement, eating disorders, marital/sexual issues and traumatic incidents. Some counsellors specialise in particular problem areas and there are a number of different approaches, which you should ask them about before you decide who to see. You don't have to have a *problem* to gain benefit from seeing a counsellor. He/she will also be able to explore ways of increasing your full potential and being more mentally and emotionally fit than you are now. See the Quick Reference section on page 107 for contact details of national organisations.

# 10 Organise yourself

*Do or do not. There is no 'try'*
Yoda, Jedi master, *Star Wars*, 1970s

You can relax more effectively if you organise yourself properly. Get yourself into some good habits which have an impact on everything you do – whether it's digging the garden or designing a space probe. Adopt some new tactics. The following are some of the ways in which successful stress-beaters make their own lives easier.

## Manage your time

Often a little forward planning saves you hours later. A lot of this chapter is devoted to thinking ahead and planning your strategy, your journey, your day, your week, your life so that you give yourself the best possible chance of achieving what you want in the time available. Following these ideas can create extra time in your life which you wouldn't have thought possible.

### 1. Make a list

List everything you have to do, today, or this week, and add to it as you think of more things. Getting a list of actions down on paper or on your computer focuses your mind and helps you to think more clearly about how and when you are going to achieve them. Once they're listed, you don't have to waste lots of energy trying to find places in your brain to park them all. Prioritise them and deal with them in order of importance. Cross things off the list as you achieve them – a satisfying reward in itself.

## 2. CUT through your week

As you go through your week, write down everything you do and how long it takes. It sounds like a chore, but it'll pay off. When you've done that, look at your list and decide which are crucial (C), which are useful (U) and which are timewasters (T).

Now look again at your timewasters. List each one and the action you will take to reduce them or cut them out altogether.

## 3. Manage your interruptions

This works well in an office environment, but can be adapted to all walks of life. If you have something important to do or to finish, ask a colleague to cover for you. Let them take all your calls, see all your visitors, etc., while you have peace and quiet. Then do the same for your colleague. Some offices have a formalised 'red and green flag' system, where half the staff, with red flags on their desks, cannot be disturbed, while the other half, with green flags, deal with 'interruptions'. At midday, they swap.

## 4. Take control of emails

Technology demands we deal with everything immediately, but how realistic is this? Open your emails at regular times during the day – once or five times depending on what suits you.

## 5. Switch off your mobile phone

It's tempting for you – and for everyone else – to feel that you're available at all times. But you don't have to be. Deliberately give yourself time and space when you can't be reached, such as while you're travelling, finishing an important piece of work, or just when you want to take a break. Most things will wait an hour or two. What's the worst that can happen?

### 6. Don't put off 'til tomorrow

Whatever unpleasant tasks you need to do, do them now. Putting them off makes them more powerful and stressful. They hang around to haunt you. Draw yourself up to your full height, take a deep breath, and get in there. One step at a time. Then give yourself a reward for having got on with it.

### 7. My problem? Or whose . . .?

The postman mistakenly puts a letter through your letter box. It's addressed to someone you've never heard of, on the other side of town. What do you do? Get your car out? Look at the local street-map? Ride around until you find the right address, and post the letter? Of course not. You helpfully and pleasantly give it back to the postman – because you both recognise that it's his problem.

Yet so often, in other situations, you take on responsibilities and problems that are not yours. Ask yourself, when you start to tackle a problem – 'Is it really my problem?' If it isn't, give it back. You can still be helpful and co-operative but without taking it all on board and owning it. Some people may not like it and may need a bit more convincing than the postman. But it's worth it for your own health and sanity. If you're constantly rescuing people from what are rightfully *their* problems you build up your stress levels and ensure that the rescued ones stay helpless.

## Set realistic goals

'I want to change my life,' I've heard people say. Fine, but what does that really mean? If your goal isn't SMART, then it's unlikely to happen.

**S** pecific
**M** easurable
**A** chievable
**R** ealistic
**T** rackable

Let's change the first statement into a SMART goal.

'So, how specifically do you want to change your life?'
*'I want to start by losing some weight.'* (Specific)

'How much weight do you want to lose – and by when?'
*'Ten pounds – before my summer holiday.'* (Measurable)

'Can you do that? Are you giving yourself long enough? Do you have a diet plan?'
*'Yes, the doctor has given me a high fibre diet with which I can lose a pound a week. I have long enough.'* (Achievable)

'What about all those business lunches you attend? Can you really stick to a diet?'
*'Yes, I shall watch carefully what I eat at lunchtime and I'll have salads and fruit, which are usually an option.'* (Realistic)

'How will you check your progress to your goal?'
*'I'll weigh myself every Friday evening before I go to bed.'* (Trackable)

Actively check out your goals in the same way. If you leave them unspecific, woolly and passive, they'll just lurk around and give you a sense of dissatisfaction.

# By the inch, it's a cinch . . . by the yard, it's hard

Notice something else about the example above. It takes the goal down to a small enough chunk to handle – from 'changing my life' to 'losing weight'. Other chunks might be changing jobs, spending more time with the children, getting fit, or learning to play the piano. Manageable chunks are a key to success in achieving your goal.

## Brainstorming

If you have what seems an insoluble problem, brainstorm possible solutions. Get a friend or a colleague to help you. Let the ideas flow thick and fast, no matter how far-fetched. Don't censure them at this first stage. This is the way to open up the creative right side of your brain.

Include solutions like:

- leave the country
- go for a pizza
- buy a canoe
- fly to Mars
- become a monk
- stand on my head
- take up trampolining
- cycle round Macclesfield
- make a film
- give away all my money.

Escape from the normal practical world you live in and be really creative. Many great inventors and artists have come up with wonderful new ideas and solutions through this brainstorming method. And the process is refreshing, stimulating and fun.

Then look at the options. What seems the most likely route to success? The answer may involve your talking to someone, asking for help or giving an unpopular message. Rehearse the solution with your friend or colleague. Get them to help you role-play, so that you feel more confident about facing the real problem head-on.

# 11 Refresh - relieve - relax

This section is a collection of relaxation ideas which have worked for me and for other people I've talked to. They don't necessarily fall into categories and I decided to be relaxed about classifying them into groups and just to offer them to you instead. Pick them up, look at them and try them out for yourself. They include some ideas for dealing with special situations – particular day to day circumstances in which many people find it hard to relax e.g. driving, going for interviews.

## Stroke your pet

Studies carried out in the USA show that for people who have had heart problems, owning and caring for a pet can reduce blood pressure and calm the body down. People with acute anxiety have also benefited greatly from their relationship with their pet. So how does it work?

First, the experience of touching and stroking or patting your pet induces a calming of the physiological processes which make you feel anxious. It can feel almost hypnotic. Touching and stroking is something we don't do much of with other humans; we often fear the response we might get from taking a friend's hand or stroking their arm. No such problems with our animal friends!

*Animals are such agreeable friends – they ask no questions, they pass no criticism*
George Eliot, author, 1819–1880

Second, you can build a close relationship of trust and affection with your pet, and you can tell him your problems, without fear of being judged or ridiculed.

Watch your pet relaxing. If you have a cat, notice how he stretches his body out and how easily and calmly he breathes, from the diaphragm. Animals are nearer to nature than we are; they are more instinctive and intuitive. No matter what animal you watch, you'll learn something if you take the time.

## Let the sun shine down on you

You probably know a bit about Seasonal Adjustment Disorder (SAD). This is where people feel sad, lethargic and depressed in the winter, when it's dark and grey. Get out into the sunshine whenever you can, even if you take your work outside with you. But remember that relaxed, well-balanced people carry around their own weather. So it doesn't have to be dismal and dreary in January. You don't have to get hooked into the annual moan. You can choose to change your outlook.

## The fishtank

It's no coincidence that dentists have tropical fish swimming around in tanks in their waiting rooms. The fact is, it's very relaxing watching fish swim lazily round in a colourful tank full of water, weeds and gravel. Just watching is soporific and can really calm you down. Let yourself merge into their underwater world for fifteen or twenty minutes. Imagine you're underwater with the fish, far away from the madding crowds. The fluidity and silence is so refreshing and calming. If you haven't got your own fishtank, visit your local petshop and amble around and gaze at the wonderful movements and colours of the aquarium. Lots of people have told me what inner stillness they get from this experience. It can work for you.

# Watch and listen

Some time ago I watched a short video sequence on TV. It showed a father lying in a meadow with his two young children. Whenever the weekend was sunny, the three of them would come to this spot, lie down and get themselves comfortable. Then they would have two minutes' silence, looking up at the clouds, listening to the sounds of the grass, the birds, the insects, planes in the distance. They concentrated hard on taking in every experience. No one was allowed to speak until the time was up.

It was quite clear that both father and children really enjoyed the experience, and found it enjoyable and peaceful. It was a shared, fun time which they looked forward to and which strengthened the bond within the family group.

## Get it out of your system

Not everyone feels comfortable sharing their problems with another person and yet it can lighten the load. In the same way, writing down some of the things that are nagging at you can be a huge help. Has someone really upset and irritated you, and it still eats away at you? Maybe it's something that happened a long time ago, and yet it's still exerting control over your feelings, and disturbing your peace of mind.

Write down all the details of the problem. What happened, when it happened, how it made you feel then and how you feel now. If it's a person who has caused you a problem, write them a letter. Tell them your feelings. Everything. Explain in full detail exactly what they did to upset you, and how that makes you feel. Be as honest and brutal as you like. Don't stop writing until you've poured it all out of your system.

Read what you've written as many times as you like. Then screw it up and throw it in the bin. Or flush it down the toilet. Or burn it. Watch it disappear and with it all those destructive feelings you've been bottling up for so long.

*I never travel without my diary. One should always have something sensational to read on the train*
Oscar Wilde, author, 1854–1900

## Start a 'smile file'

Make a list of all the things in your life you are thankful for. List anything which makes you happy. Some suggestions: family, friends, sense of humour, ability to mend things, nice teeth, good health, green fingers, enjoyment of a hobby or sport, nimble fingers, good eyesight/hearing, a loyal pet, being a good listener, a comfortable home, good food. Buy a file or folder to keep the list safe. Once it's in your 'smile file' you can look at it as often as you like.

## List your achievements

Carrying on with the positive theme, make a list – a good long one – of all your achievements. Include everything you have achieved since childhood. Examples: learning to tie my shoe-laces, passing an exam, planting a garden, learning to drive, giving a speech at a wedding, learning to ride a bike, helping a sick friend, cooking a curry, changing a fuse, mending the lawnmower, giving birth, raising a family, flying abroad, learning a language, writing a poem, scoring a goal, making a dress, getting a job, throwing a party, adopting a stray cat, mastering a computer, painting a picture, decorating the kitchen, getting fitter, growing parsley from seed, working on my stress levels.

Keep working on this list until you have at least 100 achievements. Keep going, even if you think that some of the things on the list are obvious – things that everyone does. Believe me, if you produce this list, it will give you a tremendous boost when you're feeling a bit lacking in confidence: Put it in your 'smile file' and update it regularly. You'll be surprised what a uniquely and genuinely talented individual you are!

## Brainstorm solutions

When you've got a problem and you don't know what to do about it, write down as many possible solutions as you can think of. Don't just put sensible ones – brainstorm anything that comes into your head and write it down before you make judgements about how practical they might be. Be as deliberately outlandish and off-the-wall as you can. Get a friend to help – you'll spark ideas off each other.

## Praise generously

Look for the good things which people do and let them know how much you appreciate them. We are a bit reserved when it comes to telling others that we value them. Consequently many of us don't realise just how valuable we are. Try giving praise when it's due and see how good it makes you and the other person feel.

## Switch off - literally

When I'm running Stress Management Workshops for companies, I often ask participants how they switch off after a day's work. More often than not, their way of doing this is tied to an actual physical act. For example:

- Locking the day's work securely in a drawer
- Switching off the light
- Pulling down the blinds
- Switching on the answerphone
- Washing the tea mug
- Washing your hands of the day's work
- Clocking out
- Hanging up the car keys
- Taking off a tie
- Putting on a track suit.

People tell me that they link this everyday physical action with the thought that this is the end of the work, and the action reinforces the feeling of switching off each day. This is a fine example of a physical *anchor* – linking an action to a positive thought process. What you're doing is grooving out a channel in the brain to send messages to the body that it can relax after a period of effort. What physical actions can you find in your day which will anchor your time of relaxation? Even for a short time?

## Love yourself - treat yourself

Some of us – and this can apply particularly if you are a parent – think we are being selfish if we're not constantly running around after other people, seeing to their washing, feeding them, ferrying them to discos, cleaning their rooms, and doing 1001 things which they take for granted you've been planted on this earth to do. Whether you are a parent or not, you'll no doubt find yourself sacrificing your time and energies to other people when you'd really like some time to yourself, to do what *you* want.

Make sure you give yourself love and respect by treating yourself to something you enjoy too. Life will go on in the family if you have your weekly night out with the girls, buy yourself that set of golf clubs, go for a swim, play with your model trains, have a morning in bed, read a steamy novel or sit in a bathful of bubbles occasionally. You're giving yourself positive messages that you are a valuable person in your own right. Others will be reminded of that fact too, which is no bad thing.

If you're a carer, who devotes a large part of your life to caring for an elderly relative, for example, this message applies to you more than most. It isn't selfish to think of yourself and indulge in something which brings you pleasure.

You can't take care of others effectively unless you take care of yourself.

## A verse to stick on the wall over the bath

*Somehow I was taught*
*That I should always be doing something*
*Doing nothing is usually associated with wickedness*
*'The Devil makes work for idle hands'*
*Yet I can't help thinking*
*That life would be better*
*If I knew how to rest both mind and body*
*If I knew how to do nothing, comfortably*
– Anonymous

# Some special situations

The advice above can be applied to many situations, – whichever aspects of life you might find particularly stressful. Here are some more targeted strategies.

### In the car

Sitting for long periods of time in one position puts a lot of stress on your mind and body. Give yourself the best possible time by adjusting your seat to its most comfortable position, making sure that at cruising speed your upper arms drop from your shoulders as vertically as possible. Make sure your pedals are near enough to your feet so that you are neither cramped up nor stretching out to reach them.

Check that your forehead and jaw are relaxed and keep checking while you're driving. Be conscious of your posture. Keep your head balanced gently on your shoulders, drop your shoulders, and keep your chin parallel to the floor. Feel the silver thread running up the length of your back, through the back of your neck and up to the crown of your head. Be aware of the thread being pulled gently up towards the sky, lengthening your seated body and creating space between your vertebrae. It's really worth taking a few moments before you switch on the ignition to give your body this extra space; all too often we just throw ourselves into the car, belt up and roar off. Even a minor discomfort, such as the back of the seat not being at exacdy the right angle, will be magnified over your journey and add to your feelings of stress during and after it. Car seats are not always designed to support your back properly. Invest in a lumbar support cushion to give you maximum comfort. Looking after your back is vital. It is the centre of your physical being and needs supporting properly if it is to support you.

Have you ever noticed how you are higher up in the rear view mirror first thing in the morning than last thing at night? The difference is the amount you allow your spine to be squashed down during the day. Keep it mobile by wriggling and flexing your spine during the drive. On a long journey get out of the car every hour and a half, and if possible, lie down on the grass verge to rest your back.

Walk about a bit to stretch cramped legs; rotate your shoulders backwards and forwards three or four times and move your arms in several different directions – pretend you're swimming breaststroke, crawl and backstroke – and stretch your fingers. Move your head from side to side and stretch the muscles at the back of your neck by gently moving your chin towards your chest. Place your hands on the back of your waist and stretch backwards a little, like so ) to compensate for the ( shaped position you sit in. I do exercises at service stations and laybys regularly on long journeys and have long got over any embarrassment about being watched. One or two people have asked me if I am an athlete, and are rather impressed by the performance!

As you travel along you will release stress hormones – adrenaline – when you meet an unexpected situation. Maybe you have to put the brakes on quickly to avoid someone moving out in front of you. ECG records of people who have experienced near accidents are similar to those of heart attack survivors! You also release adrenaline when you accelerate to overtake. Make a conscious effort to lengthen your breathing and let go of unnecessary tension after these incidents, to calm your body and mind. Otherwise your blood pressure will rise, the strain will build up and you'll feel stressed and tired.

One thing you can rely on when you're travelling in the car is that there'll be a hold-up. Being held up, whether you're travelling to a business meeting or trying to get to the seaside for the day, can lead to mega-stress. Remember – you choose how much stress you put on yourself in this situation. You can be the Type A personality who tenses up, grits his teeth, bangs his fist on the steering wheel and toots and swears, or you can be Type B, who listens to the radio play, puts on a CD, exercises his back and shoulders, reads the papers . . . If time is really crucial for you, if you have a business meeting, for example, then a mobile phone is invaluable. Most people experience hold-ups these days and will sympathise with you.

Leave plenty of time for delays. Your drive will be relatively carefree and you'll still have time to stop on the way/ have a wash when you get there/ read those important documents before the meeting/ have a coffee/ have a catnap in the cafe car-park. And if you're not a very confident driver, treat yourself to a couple of refresher lessons to take away some of that anxiety.

## Managing children on journeys

Taking children on long journeys – or even short ones – needs planning in advance if you're to avoid arriving at your destination like a limp rag. Organise plenty of interesting games and puzzles. For the literary, try the Alphabet game – name a flower/country/TV programme/part of the body beginning with A, then B, C, D, etc. Have plenty of colouring books and crayons, wordsearches, I-spy nature books. Think creatively. Friends who recently came to stay bought two cheap T-shirts and the two children wound string round different sections during the three-hour journey. They tie-dyed the T-shirts blue when they arrived, dried them, then spent the journey home tying them again in different places, for a pink coloured dye when they arrived home. Sounds complicated? Not really – it took a bit of forward planning and they were kept amused for hours. Hardly any 'Are we nearly there yet?'s. And the T-shirts look spectacular!

Take lots of drinks and eats with you for yourself and the children, and include lots of breaks to provide variety and exercise.

*There are two classes of travel: first-class and with children*
Robert Benchley, journalist, 1889–1945

## At the bus stop

Stand well, with your weight evenly balanced on both feet, your knees holding your legs in easy tension, your back gently upright and your shoulders dropped. Practise some neck and shoulder exercises. In these health-conscious days, it doesn't look nearly as eccentric as you might think. Bring your attention to your breathing, lengthen each breath slightly for five breaths in and out, then allow yourself to breathe easily, feeling the tension flowing out through the bottom of your feet with each out-breath. Use the waiting time to remember that wonderful holiday you had in the country, or to imagine having a cup of tea, with your feet up, and the newspaper. Tune into your music and let it transport you away, or learn a new language, a bit each day.

Look at your fellow queuers. If you're naturally inquisitive and interested in people, spend ten seconds taking in what they look like, then imagine their life stories. Where do they live? With whom? Where do they go on holiday? What do they read? Pets? TV programmes? Family? Childhood? You may never know whether you're right, but it's fun people-spotting, and it increases your awareness of your own preconceptions and prejudices. So it's good for self-development too! I often ask participants on my counselling skills workshops to do this exercise in the evening. One group who found themselves in the local hotel on the first evening of a two-day workshop ended up asking their 'victims' how accurate they were, and having a lot of fun in the process.

## In the supermarket

Don't rush. Think of it as a pleasurable experience where you are replenishing your energy as well as your cupboards. Every time you take an item off the shelf, breathe in, out and relax. Notice what other people have in their trolleys and imagine what their lifestyle is. My trolley full of catfood and wine must speak volumes! If you hate supermarket shopping go online and save yourself the time and trouble, or allow yourself to buy a treat to enjoy when you get home – some fresh crusty bread, ice-cream, flowers, herb tea, a magazine or an exotic fruit.

If you tend to panic in supermarkets, or in any other crowded or confined space, take heart. There are many people who feel just as you do, but many have overcome their panic by deliberately stopping still and taking long slow breaths. If you know you have a tendency to panic, and the symptoms are severe, take a small brown paper bag into the supermarket with you, and when you begin to feel panicky, breathe into and out of the bag. Breathing in the carbon dioxide which you have just breathed out will counteract the excess oxygen which leads to hyper-ventilation and dizziness – and more panic! So it calms your body down and restores your feelings of control. Once you know that you can do something about your panic feelings, you lose your fear, and the problem subsides and eventually disappears.

## On the telephone

Talking on the telephone can be a fraught and stressful experience. After all, you are disturbed from whatever you are doing by loud, insistent noises which won't stop until you pick up the receiver. Often a call comes at the most inconvenient time, yet you feel obliged to snap to it.

Make a habit of practising your breathing exercises (see earlier) when you're on the phone, whether you're making the call or receiving it. Put a red sticker under the receiver, so that every time you pick it up there's a trigger to remind you to relax. Position your phone within easy reach of your desk or chair, so that you are not stretching unnaturally or craning your neck. Never sit or stand with the phone jammed between your shoulder and ear. Think of the tension you are creating for yourself. Ask your caller to wait while you sit or stand comfortably – this could be a long call. If it is, stretch and wriggle from time to time to allow the blood to flow freely through your muscles.

Give yourself time and space. If someone is ringing to ask you to give up your time or take on additional work and you're really not sure you want to do it, don't be tempted to agree just because you have been caught on the hop. Feeling pressurised by an insistent caller can lead you to make bad decisions. Few things are so desperately urgent that they need an immediate response. Ask for thinking time; tell them you'll call them back. Don't apologise. Say, 'I have to go now, but I'll let you know my answer tomorrow.' This is all about you taking back *control* – which reduces your stress.

Be assertive about your time. If you are in a rush, tell your caller you have five minutes, and stick to it. This will give them a clear message about your needs and will encourage them to get to the point quickly.

When you finish your call, stand up and move your limbs and muscles before the next call. After a particularly difficult call, go and wash your hands. Ceremonially wash the caller's bad vibes down the sink before you start again.

### Before a difficult meeting or interview

Maybe you're going to have to give someone bad news, which will upset them or disappoint them. Maybe it's something you need to do to make your own life less stressful in the long run, like telling a relative you can't visit them every week any more, or you don't want to babysit for the neighbour every Saturday night. Or maybe you're attending a meeting where you're giving a presentation and people are going to ask you awkward questions afterwards.

Preparation is the essence. Remember the four Ps:

- Preparation
- Prevents
- Poor
- Performance.

Plan what you are going to say. Rehearse with a friend or colleague. Think of what problems might come up and how you are going to respond to them. Visualise yourself handling the meeting successfully. See the other people in your mind's eye, appreciating your contribution and recognising you in the most appropriate way, whether by smiling, applause, or an understanding nod.

If you're going for an interview, planning is essential. Go to the library and mug up on the 100 most popular interview questions. Find out all you can about the company. Wear your favourite smart clothes, including your most luxurious underwear. Feel good from the inside out. Treat yourself to a facial/manicure/leg wax/sauna. Whether it's an interview or not, include in your plan a treat for yourself afterwards. Reward yourself for facing up to the challenge and allowing yourself to grow.

## The stress diary

Keep a diary for a week. Write down all the things you do every day. And the things that are on your mind. Then review it at the end of the week. What are the things that are causing you the most hassle or anxiety? What can you do to make them less painful? Do you have to do them/think about them in the first place? Are they your problems? Can someone help you?

## Today – tomorrow

Think about ways of making *today* and *tomorrow* easier for yourself. For example, when can you tap into your own resourceful state? Ask a work colleague for support? Be more assertive about the use of your time? Can the family help you a bit more? Will some time to yourself help? Some physical relaxation, breathing or exercise? A treat to remind yourself how important you are?

Plan it right now. The present is all you've got.

Remember:

Stress is positive when *you're in* control.

Stress is negative when *it's* in control.

Don't forget to reward yourself for good progress!

## Instant stress busters

- emergency stop breath
- visit your mental refuge
- think of what you were worried about a year ago
- use positive affirmations – 'Every day in every way, I am getting better and better'
- stretch out – keep your blood supply running smoothly
- massage your shoulders
- step outside yourself and look at the problem objectively
- concentrate all your bodily tension into one fist, then shake it out vigorously
- ask yourself: 'What is the worst that can happen?'

## Keep it up

Being aware of your stressors and the way they affect you is the first step towards relaxing. Think of the places where you feel least relaxed. At work . . . in the kitchen . . . in the car. Buy a set of coloured stickers from the stationery shop and stick them inside your drawer at work, inside the kitchen cupboards, on the steering wheel of your car. They will be a constant reminder of your favourite strategies for relaxing and dealing with stress. As soon as you see a sticker, get into the habit of dropping your shoulders, slowing your breathing, giving yourself some positive affirmations, changing a negative thought into a positive one. You'll be helping yourself to make these responses second nature, and you won't need the stickers after a while.

## Congratulate yourself

Now that you have almost finished this book, sit back and reflect on what you have learned. What are you doing differently already which is making a difference to your life and to those around you? What will you do next? Congratulate yourself every time you deal with a difficult situation more effectively. Give yourself a pat on the back for starting off on your new path to a fulfilling life.

> *Relax. Surround yourself now with the people and things that reflect who you are and who you want to be.*

# Quick reference 1: Ideas from friends and colleagues

These are some quick pick-me-ups that work for people I know:

'Going to the cinema is an escape; you're in another world. It's always enjoyable and relaxing.'

'A game of cards and a few drinks with friends every Saturday night helps me forget the troubles of the week. The card game makes me concentrate on something different and I have a good laugh with my mates.'

'When I feel down, I put on a piece of music which reflects my mood. I allow my emotions to come right up to the surface and then to flood out. Often this means I have a real good cry. Afterwards, I feel that I have got rid of a lot of negative stress and I feel better for it.'

'I throw myself into the housework. I polish and shine everything in sight. Sometimes I feel physically exhausted. But I always feel proud of what I've done, when I sit back and look at it. It gives me back a sense of achievement.'

'Jogging has been a life-saver to me, in times of stress. I don't know how I would have got through some of the difficult times if I hadn't had that hour for myself every day, when I could just run and run . . .'

'I sort out the shed/loft/garage. Throwing out the rubbish is like throwing away your problems. I feel like a new person afterwards.'

'Cooking is my relaxation. Blending all those interesting ingredients together, and experimenting with new ideas of my own, is very satisfying. Even though I'm physically and mentally tired, I'm too restless to just sit in front of the TV at night. Creating a good meal after work is my way of winding down.'

'When someone makes me feel intimidated, scared or bored, I put my head on one side, smile slightly, assume a "listening" pose and then I say to myself, *"What you don't know is that I'm actually doing my pelvic floor exercises."* And I do.'

'I ring my best friend when things get on top of me. He listens and lets me talk. He is supportive when I need support and gives me a practical jolt when I need it. Even though he doesn't always agree with everything I do or say, I know he's on my side. I do the same for him when he's fed up.'

'On a dark night I watch the stars. The size of the universe makes me and my problems seem very small. It also works when I'm near the coast and I look out to sea.'

'I shut myself in the bathroom for half an hour, and have a long soak in a bubble-bath. No one is allowed to disturb me, except if the house is burning down.'

'I put on my favourite music – really loud – and dance.'

'Taking the dog out for a long walk works for me – it helps to get things back in perspective.'

'I play sports whenever I can. Competing against others or against my personal best gives me a sense of achievement and makes me feel fit and positive. I can use this time to get myself into peak condition for when I get work.'

'Doing voluntary work with the elderly and ill gives me a sense of being valued. It also reminds me how lucky I am to be young and fit.'

'Going to the gym in the morning before work channels my energies for the task ahead. When I go after work, it takes care of all those left-over frustrations.'

'Having a good sing in the choir takes me off into another world. The strings of unknown notes are a real challenge and there's a sense of achievement when they're mastered. There's the physical exercise and relaxation I get from the breathing, and, most importantly, the friendship of the three other warblers I meet for a meal and a drink and a laugh before rehearsals.'

# Quick reference 2: Resources

This section provides you with contact details for organisations mentioned earlier.

## Relaxing activities

### Alexander Technique

The Society of Teachers of the Alexander Technique
0845 230 7828
www.stat.org.uk

### General relaxation classes

The Relaxation for Living Institute
020 7439 4277
www.relaxationforliving.co.uk

### Massage therapy

The General Council for Massage Therapy
0870 850 4452
www.gcmt.org.uk

### Yoga

The British Wheel of Yoga
01529 306 851
www.bwy.org.uk

# Counsellors and therapists

### ACAT - Cognitive Analytical Therapy

0844 800 9496
www.acat.me.uk

### British Association for Behavioural and Cognitive Psychotherapies

0161 797 4484
www.babcp.com

### British Association for Counselling and Psychotherapy

01455 88 3300
www.bacp.co.uk

### UKCP Home

0207 014 9955
www.psychotherapy.org.uk

# Helplines

Action on Addiction (addiction)
0845 126 4130
www.actiononaddiction.org.uk

Alcoholics Anonymous (alcohol addiction)
0845 769 7555
www.alcoholics-anonymous.org.uk

Al-Anon (for family and friends of problem drinkers)
020 7403 0888
www.al-anonuk.org.uk

Anxiety Alliance (phobias, panic attacks, OCD)
0845 296 7877
www.anxietyalliance.org.uk

Careline (any subject)
0845 1228 622
www.ukselfhelp.info/careline

Childline (child abuse and neglect)
0800 1111
www.childline.org.uk

Cruse (bereavement)
0844 477 9400
www.crusebereavementcare.org.uk

Depression Alliance (depression)
0845 123 2320
www.depressionalliance.org

Drugsline (drug or alcohol addiction)
0808 1606 606
www.drugsline.org

London Lesbian & Gay Switchboard (sexuality)
020 7837 7324
www.llgs.org.uk

MacMillan Cancer Support (cancer)
0808 808 2020
www.macmillan.org.uk

MIND (mental health issues)
0845 766 0163
www.mind.org.uk

NHS Direct (round-the-clock health advice)
0845 4647
www.nhsdirect.nhs.uk

National Centre for Domestic Violence
(legal support for victims of domestic violence)
08709 220704
www.ncdv.org.uk

National Centre for Eating Disorders
(anorexia, bulimia and other eating disorders)
01372 469 493
www.eating-disorders.org.uk

Parentline (parental problems)
0808 800 2222
www.parentlineplus.org.uk

Relate (relationships and sexuality)
0845 456 1310
www.relate.org.uk

Samaritans (suicidal thoughts, distress, despair)
08457 909090
www.samaritans.org

Terrence Higgins Trust (HIV/AIDS)
0845 1221 200
www.tht.org.uk

# Quick reference 3: Further reading

Axt, P and Axt-Gadermann, M *The Joy of Laziness* London: Bloomsbury, 2005

Baker, R *Understanding Panic Attacks* Oxford: Lion Hudson, 2003

Dyer, W *You'll See It When You Believe It* London: Arrow, 2005

Ferguson J *Perfect Confidence* London: Random House Books, 2009

Field, L *Be Yourself* London: Vermillion, 2003

Floyd, E *1001 Little Healthy Eating Miracles* London: Carlton, 2008

Hay, L *You Can Heal Your Life* London: Hay House, 2004

Herbert, C and Wetmore, A *Overcoming Traumatic Stress* London: Constable & Robinson, 1999

Hilton, J *Busy Person's Guide to Stress Relief* London: Gaia, 2006

Johnson, S *Who Moved My Cheese?* London: Vermilion, 1999

Marriott, S *1001 Ways to Relax* London: DK, 2008

Weller, S *The Better Back Book* London: Hamlyn, 2005

Williamson, K *Sleep Deep* New York: Penguin Group, 2007

# Notes

# Perfect Confidence

## Jan Ferguson

### All you need to get it right first time

- Do you find it hard to stay calm under pressure?
- Are you worried that you don't always stand up for yourself?
- Do you want some straightforward advice on overcoming insecurities?

*Perfect Confidence* is the ideal companion for anyone who wants to boost their self-esteem. Covering everything from communicating clearly to handling conflict, it explains exactly why confidence matters and equips you with the skills you need to become more assertive. Whether you need to get ahead in the workplace or learn how to balance the demands of friends and family, *Perfect Confidence* has all you need to meet challenges head on.

The *Perfect* series is a range of practical guides that give clear and straightforward advice on everything from getting your first job to choosing your baby's name. Written by experienced authors offering tried-and-tested tips, each book contains all you need to get it right first time.

BOOKS

# Perfect Positive Thinking

## Lynn Williams

### All you need to know

- Are you troubled by negative thoughts?
- Do you find it hard to get motivated?
- Would you like some guidance on how to feel more upbeat?

*Perfect Positive Thinking* is essential reading for anyone who wants to feel optimistic and enthusiastic. Written by a professional life coach, with years of experience in the field, it gives practical advice on how to overcome negative feelings, explains how to deal with problems like anxiety and self-doubt, and provides helpful tips on how to gain energy, motivation and a sense of purpose. Covering everything from exercising to eating, and from stretching to sleep, *Perfect Positive Thinking* has all you need to feel happy and confident.

BOOKS